① anti-strictness - 4, 88, 1086
② needed distinctions among "strict" churches - 24, 28, 121

37₆ - ecological support

47 - origins of an SBC cong in CA is displaced
51   southerners, to some extent

53 - a bit washy-washy on meaning of "southern" -
     sometimes refers to the cultural south and
     sometimes to a cultural style.

58 - need to distinguish tween literally southern
     denoms (eg SBC) + a religious style that
     may live in other denoms - "southernization"
     thesis seems better re second than first

③ can paint the case studies as portraits
   independent of their status as evidence for
   the southernization thesis

83 - maybe say are 2 branches of E - southern +
                                    nonsouthern?

90 - "southern religion" gets, defined as cultural
     form, may not be prominent anymore in the south

④ 91 - describe book as instantiate of classic soc.?
       cul. theme of how religion + society interact

91 - regional diff's sometimes conflated with
     firm time dimension (southern = old)

92 - evangelical growth ≠ increased cultural
                         conservatism

Amer
relig

① diffusn of southern religious style as one
source of emergent to E. More generally,
sensitive to regional base?

② 4 case studies are intrinsically
interesting documentation of variation
among contemp Es.

③ sensitive to cultural variation
within E

(maybe make ② + ③ two aspects of same
point)

Resurgent Evangelicalism
in the United States

Resurgent Evangelicalism in the United States

Mapping Cultural Change since 1970

Mark A. Shibley

UNIVERSITY OF SOUTH CAROLINA PRESS

Copyright © 1996 University of South Carolina

Published in Columbia, South Carolina, by the
University of South Carolina Press

Manufactured in the United States of America

00 99 98 97 96   5 4 3 2 1

Library of Congress Cataloging-in-Publication Data

Shibley, Mark A., 1961–
   Resurgent Evangelicalism in the United States : mapping cultural
change since 1970 / Mark A. Shibley
     p.   cm.
   Includes bibliographical references and index.
   ISBN 1–57003–106–1
   1. Evangelicalism—United States—History—20th century.
2. United States—Church history—20th Century. I. Title.
BR1642.U5S456   1996
280'.4'097309045—dc20   95–50218

For Barbara and Gilbert Shibley,
my greatest teachers,
and in memory of my grandmother,
a true believer.

Contents

Tables

Preface

The most visible recent development in American religion has been the resurgence of born-again Christianity, and the high profile of this movement's political wing—the New Christian Right—has led sympathizers and detractors alike to misinterpret the meaning of resurgent evangelicalism and its effect on the wider culture. This book explains how and why evangelical Protestantism has regained nationwide prominence in the later half of the twentieth century, and by examining regional differences in American religion and culture, I show that resurgent evangelicalism does not signal a liberal-to-conservative shift in American morality so much as it represents the further privatization of religious life in the United States. That is, evangelical Protestantism is increasingly popular among individual seekers but continues to diminish as a legitimating force in public life. My findings are based on an analysis of church membership trends nationwide, nine months of participant observation in several evangelical congregations in California and the Midwest, and representative individual-level data from the National Opinion Research Center's General Social Survey.

I would like to thank a number of people and institutions who made this work possible. First, the Department of Sociology at the University of California–Santa Barbara, an intellectually stimulating and professionally nurturing place whose faculty, including Rich Appelbaum, Harvey Molotch, Clark Roof, Bruce Straits, and John Sutton, were very supportive and greatly informed the early stages of this research. I especially thank faculty member Phil Hammond, a first-rate scholar, brilliant teacher, and friend of many years. His guidance and generosity were invaluable to me.

Second, I would like to thank the Department of Sociology and Anthropology at Loyola University–Chicago, my current academic home. Several of my Loyola colleagues read portions of the manuscript and provided moral support, especially Kathleen Adams, Anne Figert, Fred Kniss, Phil Nyden, and Judy Wittner. Jon Wiggins has been my thoughtful and energetic research assistant.

Third, I must thank Ben Johnson, a dear friend and mentor. His inspired teaching in an undergraduate sociology of religion course at the University of Oregon in 1983 started me down the vocational path that led to the writing of this book. His early comments on southern religion and the history of American evangelicalism have given, I hope, conceptual clarity to the project. This manuscript has benefited from conversations with many other sociologists of religion, including Mimi Goldman, Paul Kennedy, Don Miller, and Robin Perrin.

Finally and most important, I want to thank the born-again Christians who welcomed me into their congregations.

Resurgent Evangelicalism
in the United States

Introduction
Understanding Resurgent Evangelicalism

For more than twenty years observers of American culture have documented and interpreted the resurgence of evangelical Protestantism. Its prosperity in the face of liberal Protestant decline is now a matter of record (see Kelley 1972 and Roof and McKinney 1987). Yet important questions about the origins and consequences of this shift within Protestantism remain unanswered. What, for example, are the social and cultural roots of this reinvigorated style of Protestant worship? And if, as some scholars suggest (see Hunter 1983 and Ammerman 1987), the revival of evangelicalism is essentially a reaction to the deterioration of traditional Christian morality in modern culture—that is, a fundamentalist movement—what can be said about the future of evangelicalism and American society generally? In other words, how are we to understand the meaning of resurgent evangelicalism in late-twentieth-century America?

I address these issues by returning to the question of *how* evangelicalism has gained new prominence in recent decades, what accounts for its nationwide popularity. I answer in light of the following observation: the kind of conservative Protestantism on the rise nationally is precisely the style of Christianity that has dominated the American South culturally for almost two centuries. Understanding resurgent evangelicalism—its origins and consequences—hinges, therefore, on understanding regional differences in American religion and culture. Thus my first claim is that the reconfiguration of American Protestantism in the latter half of the twentieth century—resurgent evangelicalism and the concomitant demise of liberal congregations—is at least partly a result of the diffusion of southern-style religion into nonsouthern regions of the country. Yet over time—and this is my second claim—evangelicalism has itself been transformed. The unavoidable encounter with pluralism and profoundly secular elements of American culture outside the South has changed the form and meaning of evangelical Protestantism. Hence my two central metaphors: the southernization of American religion and the Californication of conservative Protestantism. This book assembles evidence supporting these companion propositions and considers the meaning of resurgent evangelicalism in their light.

1

From Margin to Mainstream

In the nineteenth century, to be Protestant in America was to be evangelical—a born-again Christian. In this century, however, like all traditional religion in a modern context, evangelicalism has been severely challenged. One might even say that evangelicalism lost the early battles with modernism and by mid-century was relegated to a peripheral role in American culture. The South is an exception, however. There evangelicalism maintained legitimacy vis-à-vis the wider culture. To this day, to be an evangelical Christian in the former Confederacy is more an asset than a burden in public life.

Given this history, John Egerton, a noted southern journalist, characterizes the nationwide resurgence of born-again Christianity as the spread of southern-style religion. By this he means that evangelicalism has transcended regional boundaries and moved into the mainstream of American culture. Billy Graham, Egerton writes, has "taken the old-time religion of his native South out into the nation and the world, [and] in doing so, he has firmly established himself as the single most influential figure in what can fairly be called the Southernization of American religion" (1974, 195). Since Egerton wrote these words, dozens of other prominent southern evangelicals have attained national and international reputations, largely as a result of their popularity as television evangelists (see Hadden and Swann 1981; Frankl 1987). Like the vitality of country and western music in recent years, evangelicalism, though found throughout the United States, seems to emanate from the South.

Egerton is not a lone voice. Lowell D. Streiker and Gerald S. Strober (1972), for example, portray Billy Graham as the quintessential middle American, arguing that Americans' beliefs about God and Jesus Christ are becoming increasingly like his. Samuel S. Hill Jr., foremost scholar of southern religion, invokes the southernization metaphor in a recent book on the variety of southern religious experience. He writes, "Sophisticates, secularists, and 'modern' people of one kind or another may be puzzled by southern ways and by the intensity of evangelicalism, but those features of regional culture have come to be taken for granted—indeed treated with respect—as a prominent part of American life" (1988, 2). David Edwin Harrell Jr., another student of southern religion, offers this succinct description of the relationship between resurgent evangelicalism and southern culture: "The South was a reservoir where the old-time message had remained intact amid the challenges of the twentieth century. Threatened by an intensified modernity in the postwar years, Americans looked for religious answers and Southerners had them" (1981, 3).

Indeed, by these accounts the South is a kind of repository for American evangelicalism. But how did this distinct cultural form become available to a wider, national population? More directly put, do southerners carry their religious traditions with them when they move, as they often have in this century?

In chapter 1 I sketch the history and geography of American evangelicalism and define what I mean by "southern-style religion." Chapter 2 considers the possibility that most recent evangelical growth is attributable to growth in specifically southern evangelical churches, which are growing fastest in nonsouthern regions of the country that southerners have moved into. Field work in two "southern" church settings in California—the subject matter of chapters 3 and 4—further supports the thesis that migration out of the South and the accompanying spread of southern religion is a plausible way to understand resurgent evangelicalism, at least its beginning. But the more difficult question is whether or not this distinctive Protestant style has permeated social life outside the South to the extent that it is changing American culture. That is the question I address in chapter 5. In fact, field work in southern churches outside the South suggests that the most important effect of the geographic diffusion of southern-style religion may be the transformation of evangelicalism itself. The spread of born-again Christianity is changing the face of American culture, to be sure, but it too is being changed by the process.

Southern Churches Outside the South

The South is a safe haven for evangelical Protestantism, and when southern religion moves out of its native region, the tension between it and the secular world increases. Therefore, while southernization indicates a growing acceptance of evangelicalism in mainstream America—a periphery-to-center metaphor—there is enormous pressure on southern religion to adapt to a substantially less religious culture outside the South, a challenge faced by all religious movements as they encounter the secular world. Churches that cannot find ways to accommodate the new environment will never take root in the culture and will either be marginal or perish in the long run (see Troeltsch 1976).

James Davison Hunter (1982; see especially chapter 6) argues that a major thrust of contemporary evangelicalism is the effort to accommodate modern culture: theology is becoming more rational; relations with other religious traditions are becoming more civil; and evangelical life is becoming more privatized. In keeping with Hunter's findings and my major thesis, I argue that the diffusion of southern religion is a process that intensifies evangelicalism's encounter with secular culture, and southern religion can be expected to respond in one of two ways: by resistance or by accommodation. How that process is unfolding can be seen only from inside southern churches themselves.

I have therefore studied the flagship congregations of two major southern evangelical denominations in a nonsouthern community (reported in chapters 3 and 4) and discovered that such churches, initially vital centers of evangelicalism outside the South, are now struggling to survive. They drew on a population of displaced southerners in their early years and remain "southern" in many important ways. Their experience is thus consistent with the southernization thesis; but precisely because they are antagonistic toward the surrounding culture and reaffirm old identities, and because there are other evangelical congregations in the community that "fit" the culture and are therefore healthy, the vitality of southern religion outside the South, and its success in attracting nonsoutherners, may be primarily due to its ability to adapt to pluralistic settings rather than simply the results of interregional migration.

One of the "southern" churches I studied is an affiliate of the Southern Baptist Convention (SBC), the other an Assemblies of God congregation. Both churches grew during the 1960s and 1970s, drawing heavily on people reared in a conservative Protestant tradition, particularly southerners. By 1990, however, membership was down 50 percent, and both churches were struggling financially. By contrast, evangelical churches that embrace secular elements of the surrounding culture are growing rapidly (see chapter 5). Furthermore, there are examples of people in this nonsouthern community who have left the old style of evangelicalism for the new, and there are a few well-known examples of "southern" churches that are booming outside the South precisely because they make a concerted effort to blend with contemporary lifestyles.

Why Some Evangelical Churches Are Growing

More than two decades ago Dean Kelley (1972) argued, in effect, that conservative churches grow *because* they are strict—that is, they attract and retain members because they demand complete loyalty, unwavering belief, and rigid adherence to a distinct lifestyle. That argument reverberated through twenty years of church growth research and was recently elaborated by Laurence R. Iannaccone (1994), whose rational-choice theory claims that the strength of a church is a result of its strictness. Is this true in evangelical churches outside the South?

Cultural traditionalism—moral strictness—is a characteristic feature of southern religion, and Kelley and Iannaccone observe that groups like the Southern Baptist Convention have grown dramatically relative to the old "mainline" Protestant churches. Why is this so? My field work suggests that strictness may not be the operative variable in some evangelical growth at present or in years to come. Evangelical Protestantism outside the South is gaining middle-class respectability, and those who join, particularly young people, seem to be searching for community and personal well-being. Most are not moral crusaders even if they tend to be conservative on some social issues. We need therefore to look more deeply into the social sources of contemporary evangelicalism to understand its renewed appeal. What motivates people, particularly those reared outside the tradition, to join the ranks of born-again Christians?

Following H. Richard Niebuhr's (1965) analytic strategy, chapter 7 uses national-survey data to identify the social correlates of evangelical preference, and I explore the hypothesis that this branch of American Protestantism remains a "church of the disinherited," though more in social and cultural terms that in economic ones. The inverse relationship between social class and evangelical preference has diminished over time, particularly outside the South. Moral traditionalism, on the other hand, is still salient in all regions of the United States, and it affects evangelical preference regardless of socioeconomic status. Most evangelicals, rich or poor, are culturally conservative, especially on issues of sexuality, but is that *why* they join—to preserve a traditional lifestyle?

Following clues from field work in evangelical churches outside the South, in chapter 7 I suggest that personal crisis, discontentment, and rootlessness may explain more about evangelical preference than a high degree of moral regulation, and if regional differences among conservative Protestants can be taken as a harbinger of change within the evangelical subculture, then resurgent evangelicalism is less a social reform movement than a gathering of individuals seeking community and/or cure from personal ills, be they social, psychological, physical, or spiritual.

The Meaning of Resurgent Evangelicalism

If resurgent evangelicalism is understood as the southernization of American religion—and there is good evidence to support such an understanding—then perhaps the restructuring of American religion portends deep changes in American culture. That interpretation is consistent with Robert Wuthnow's (1988) thesis that the realignment of Protestant culture is on a liberal-to-conservative axis, and it resonates with James Hunter's (1991) culture-wars thesis. However—and there is compelling evidence here as well—if conservative Protestantism must accommodate secular culture to survive in the long run, then the potential of resurgent evangelicalism—conservative southern religion—to reform the wider culture is limited. Evangelicalism outside the South, because it must accommodate to survive, will increasingly shape itself to meet individual needs first and foremost. New-style evangelicalism will emphasize attention to individual needs rather than corporate problems, and thus the *he means this is the relevant dimension, not that movement is from left → right or from [illegible]*

restructuring of American religion and culture may, in the long run, be more public-to-private than liberal-to-conservative. Obituaries of the so-called New Christian Right have been written (see Bruce 1989). Because of its sheer size, however, evangelicalism's effect on American culture will be substantial in the foreseeable future, though not in the way that the liberal cultural elite feared in the 1980s.

This interpretation—that evangelicalism is _not_ fundamentally reforming America's moral and political terrain in a socially conservative direction— hinges on attention to regional differences in America religion and culture, including variation in the reciprocal effect of regional subcultures on transplanted religious styles. When southern religion leaves the South, it changes the face of American culture and is itself changed in the process. American society generally becomes more evangelical and thus *looks* more conservative religiously, but the meaning of evangelicalism changes in that it has less moral authority outside the South. Evangelical affiliation and submission to church authority become matters of individual choice. Thus the ability of churches to meet individual needs rather than their conservative moral outlook is the defining characteristic of contemporary, resurgent evangelicalism.

Part I

The Southernization
of American Religion

.

CHAPTER ONE

A Regional History
of Evangelical Protestantism

For a century and a half . . . the American South has been
permeated by the Christian religion and dominated by one
family of that massive tradition, evangelical Protestantism.
To this day, notwithstanding the winds of secularization, natu-
ralism, and positivism, its people remain attached to the
church and responsive to religious teachings, perhaps more
so than anywhere else in Christendom.

Samuel S. Hill

Does it make sense to speak of a "southern" style of religious life in American culture today? In arguing that resurgent evangelicalism is related to the
spread of southern culture, I imply that religion in the South is somehow distinctive and that this distinctiveness is, to a degree, transportable. It is my
good fortune that scholars of American religious history have turned considerable attention to southern religion in recent years—that is, religious life *inside*
the South (see Bailey 1964; Dorough 1974; Harrell 1981; Hill 1962, 1972,
1980, 1983, 1988; Mathews 1977).[1] Ultimately, my sociological task is to show
how this cultural form transcended its regional base and moved into the mainstream of American culture—to explain southern religion *outside* the South.
To test the southernization thesis empirically, it is necessary to discuss the history and geography of conservative Protestantism in the southern United States.

There are three important points to make in this regard. First, it is clear
that evangelicalism in the South has a distinct flavor—stylistic peculiarities
that have, along with country music, redneck accents, and "down-home" cook-

---

1. The early studies of southern religion emphasize its distinctiveness (see Bailey 1964; Dorough
1974). More recent work gives attention to variety in southern religion (see Harrell 1981; Hill
1988) but also reinforces the view that southern evangelicalism is distinguishable from religious
life in other regions of the country.

9

ing, come to be identified with southern culture. Second, while evangelicalism is not uniquely southern, it survived the twentieth-century challenges of modernism in a position of cultural dominance only in the South. The fundamentalist-modernist controversy, and the South's unique history of defeat and ridicule, were pivotal in the evolution of southern-style religion. Third, despite rapid social change in the South following the Second World War, the evangelical core of southern culture remains demonstrably intact though increasingly challenged. Several recent geographic studies of American religion show, not surprisingly, that the former Confederate states are still largely evangelical (Zelinsky 1961; Shortridge 1977; Newman and Halvorson 1982), that in fact the region remains remarkably homogeneous compared to the rest of the country. While evangelicalism can be defined generally, "southern-style religion" is definable more specifically.

Culture-Protestantism in the American South

Evangelical Protestantism has a long history in the United States, and its central motifs—biblical orthodoxy, personal piety, and missionary zeal—go back at least as far as the First Great Awakening (1730–60), which began in New England with the work of Jonathan Edwards. The Second Great Awakening (1800–30), following the American Revolution, was more widespread and involved a southern and westward expansion of evangelical styles. Frontier preachers among the Baptists, Methodists, and Presbyterians were the couriers of this second wave of revivalistic Protestantism, the beginning of "folk" religion, revivals, and the camp-meeting phenomenon, all characteristic features of nineteenth-century evangelicalism. The earliest evangelical impulses in America were not, therefore, indigenous to the South.

Prior to the Civil War, many of the great waves of Protestant revival occurred in the North (for example, in upstate New York's "burned over district"); and the early generations of interdenominational itinerant evangelists were mostly northerners, among them Charles Finney, Dwight Moody, and Billy Sunday. Even the Holiness and, later, Pentecostal movements, which became very popular in the South beginning in the late nineteenth century, did not originate there. In fact, Los Angeles was the center of emergent Pentecostalism at the turn of the century. Northern evangelical circles, particularly around Southern California's Charles Fuller, were certainly an important catalyst for the modern vitality of evangelical religion (see Marsden 1987). Fuller helped discover and promote Billy Graham, for example, though he did not go south to find him; Graham came north to get educated (at Wheaton College) and moved into Fuller's circle there. In short, evangelicalism did not originate in the South, despite its current dominance in the region. How did this come about?

The introduction of evangelicalism to the southern United States is attributable to the efforts of the missionary preachers in the latter half of the eighteenth century. They introduced frontier folk to the evangelical style of worship and helped legitimate Protestant belief throughout the South by 1800, thus preparing the ground for revival and church growth in the opening decades of the nineteenth century.

The spark that ignited the South's first Great Revival, as it came to be called (I referred to it above as the Second Great Awakening), began on the banks of Kentucky's Gasper River in the summer of 1800 (Boles 1985, 23). James McGready, a Presbyterian minister, organized a large-scale interdenominational outdoor meeting—infused with revivalistic prayer and preaching—that lasted several days and excited many people. Other camp meetings were subsequently organized in other places, and McGready's successful efforts that summer set in motion a pattern of religious revival in the region.

The purpose of these gatherings was to heighten religious enthusiasm among ordinary people. The calling of missionary clergy in the expanding South and West was to "chase the devil out of the wilderness" (that is, to save souls), not debate church doctrine. Inspiring religious experience and engendering personal piety were the objectives. By 1805, the Great Revival receded, but the occurrence of camp meetings and religious excitement had by that time spread throughout much of the South (Boles 1985, 24).

Harrell's description of nineteenth-century revivalism captures nicely the constitution and texture of southern religion:

> [Revivalism in the South] produced a remarkably enduring set of characteristics. Rather than viewing the camp meetings as essentially a social event with a thin religious veneer, one should view them as the anvil upon which plain folk religion was forged. The common people who preached and exhorted without benefit of much education made folk religion democratic. The camp meeting songs, which were both rousing and easily sung, contained a coherent system of religious symbols important to frontier people. Appeal was to the heart more than to the head, and conversion was the dominant religious experience. The quest for personal holiness which followed conversion took an individualistic course; reform was inward and aimed at the individual, not outward and aimed at society. Theology was heavily laced with Calvinistic notions of the sinfulness of man and the need for repentance. Services were less liturgical, reliance on Biblical authority more complete, the importance

of good, popular preaching greater than was true among other American Protestants. These elements became the essence of southern folk religion. (1988, 27–28)

Remarkably, evangelicalism became, in the early decades of the nineteenth century, not only the popular form of religious observance among southerners but also a defining characteristic of an emerging southern culture. Evangelical religion shaped the mentality of antebellum southerners, and, Harrell writes, "by 1830 the 'Solid South' was more a religious than a political reality" (1988, 26–27). The spirit of frontier revivalism—its availability to ordinary folk because of its intellectual simplicity, its restorative and invigorating message, and its offer of reassurance and certainty—is still pervasive in southern culture today, though in modified form, and it can be observed in southern religion outside the South.

The evangelical emphasis on individual salvation and personal piety, regulated by the local congregation, had the effect of personalizing religion in the old South. Southern evangelicals in the early nineteenth century were mostly world-rejecting. Thus their commitment was to reforming individual sinners, not the world at large. Religious historian John B. Boles put it this way: "The ills of society they saw as less a legitimate social concern than the aggregate sins of numerous individuals" (1985, 27). Charles Finney's social perfectionism, associated with Protestant revivalism in the North, was therefore not part of evangelical culture in the South. However, the personalizing of religious life did not mean that southern evangelicalism was socially irrelevant during the nineteenth century. On the contrary, it came over time to dominate the region culturally and to be not only individually important but socially important as well. Evangelical hegemony in the nineteenth century represented a significant shift from colonial days, Boles notes,

> but the result was less a sense of religious community than a religious culture, to make an important distinction. During the late colonial period, in those regions where there was an established church, everyone was presumed to occupy a position in a hierarchical community determined by church and civil laws. In that context the evangelicals, with their willingness to preach anywhere at any time and with their alternative values that emphasized self-denying humility, constituted a culturally revolutionary force. (1985, 27)

But what kind of revolutionary force? That question must be asked of contemporary evangelicalism as well.

Evangelicalism in the South began as a dissenting voice, a challenge to the Anglican establishment. "Plain folk" religion emphasized experience and spontaneity rather than doctrinal education and orderliness. At its inception, this new religion of the people included a critical stance toward slavery, but the history of southern religion is a tale of how this pietistic form of Protestantism come first to be culturally pervasive and then a kind of "establishment" religion itself that eventually justified slavery.

After the initial spread of revivalistic Protestantism in the early 1800s, two events stand out as decisive in the history of American evangelicalism, but especially in the history of southern religion—the Civil War in the latter half of the last century and the fundamentalist-modernist controversy in the early part of this century. The first event was decisive because it intensified evangelicalism in the South, the second because it marginalized evangelicalism everywhere except in the South.

While evangelicalism was never this-worldly in theological terms, the South's unique history of slavery, defeat, abject poverty, and ridicule—the Civil War being the central event in this history—fundamentally reconstituted religious life in the region, blending evangelicalism into southern culture so that by the end of the nineteenth century, religion and culture among white southerners were inseparable.

The Civil War and Southern Religion

In the early decades of Protestant revival in the South, Baptists and Methodists preached the gospel to blacks and whites alike; a soul was a soul and the business of the clergy was salvation. The message—all are equal in the eyes of God—was subversive to a racially stratified society. Since many Baptists and Methodists were themselves outside the establishment, they found it easy to identify with the humanity of black slaves. As their influence spread, however, evangelicals felt increasing pressure to affirm southern society in the face of growing criticism from the North. This led eventually to compromise on the issue of slavery, setting the southern faithful apart from their abolitionist evangelical kin in the North. Boles writes,

> In exchange for the ability to grow as denominations, the quintessential southern churches gave up their critical stance toward slavery. No longer would it be addressed as a social evil; now it was seen as an inevitable, natural, and hence ordained-by-God part of southern society. . . . [Furthermore], to criticize any substantial aspect of southern society was considered tantamount to joining forces with the abolitionists. So the

evangelists, prospering in the South, were hesitant to jeopardize their position; they ended up defending southern society. (1985, 29)

By the 1820s evangelicalism lost its revolutionary edge, and, because evangelicalism emphasized personal sin and the promise of forgiveness, the structural inadequacies of the larger society could be ignored in its mission. As long as people's own houses were in order, they could be forgiven for living in an unjust society. If evangelical Protestantism had given reassurance to ordinary southerners struggling with the hardships of frontier life in the late eighteenth and early nineteenth centuries, it gave similar reassurance to southerners in the late nineteenth and early twentieth centuries who were burdened with the legacy of slavery and defeat.

The experience of defeat in the Civil War deepened evangelical faith for many white southerners and consequently preserved and intensified that Protestant tradition in the South. Kenneth K. Bailey's opening paragraph in *Southern White Protestantism in the Twentieth Century* reads as follows:

During the last dreary days of the Confederacy, a Mississippi Methodist preacher defiantly exhorted his people: "If we cannot gain our *political,* let us establish at least our *mental* independence." The preacher's plea was portentous, for the future would demonstrate that military conquest had exacted no spiritual surrender. A proud and undaunted "*mental* independence" survived and flourished among southerners—a fountain both of weakness and of strength, of cohesion and of strife. (1964, 1)

Indeed, the Civil War solidified evangelicalism as a core feature of southern identity. It helped bind white southerners to each other and to their region.

This theme—religion of the Lost Cause—is developed in Charles Reagan Wilson's study of religion and region in post-Civil War history, *Baptized in Blood* (1980). He argues that the dream of a separate southern identity did not die in 1865 with military defeat. Rather the outcome of the war ordained that southern separateness would be more a cultural than political reality. Of necessity, one vision replaced the other. According to Wilson, "the South's kingdom was to be of culture, not of politics. Religion was at the heart of this dream, and the history of the attitude known as the Lost Cause was the story of the use of the past as the basis for a Southern religious-moral identity, an identity as a chosen people. The Lost Cause was therefore the story of the linking of two profound human forces, religion and history" (1980, 1). The product of this connection, which Wilson traces through the decades following the war, is a cultural form he identifies as "southern civil religion." Wilson means that not only have the religious lives of southerners shaped the region's culture, but also evangelicalism in the South reflects, indeed conserves, the culture's history and values. Hill (1962) calls this blend of the sacred and profane the South's "culture-Protestantism."

One particularly rich and suggestive example of the intertwining of religion and culture in southern history is seen in the following excerpt from a 1927 speech by a South Carolina minister:

> To those who can read history it is unthinkable that any one fail to see in it all the hand of God bringing the many thousands from the bondage imposed upon us by social and economic forces which of ourselves we were powerless to control. . . . It is imperative that we think of Southern industry as a spiritual movement and of ourselves as instruments in a Divine plan. Southern industry is the largest single opportunity the world has ever had to build a democracy upon the ethics of Christianity. . . . Southern industry is to measure the power of Protestantism, unmolested. . . .
>
> Southern industry was pioneered by men possessing the statesmanship of the prophets of God. . . . I personally believe it was God's Way for the development of a forsaken people. (As quoted by Liston Pope 1970, 24)

Of course, the South and the place of religion in southern culture have changed after more than a half century of rapid modernization, but a pervasive evangelical legacy remains, and its present character is captured by sociologist Nancy Tatom Ammerman:

> While southern evangelicalism was never officially established, it enjoyed a privileged church-like status in Southern law and society. Blue laws established rules for Sunday conduct, and vice laws (including prohibition) gave evangelical morals legal force. Pastors routinely served as school chaplains, and Sunday School teachers populated the classrooms. No one ever seemed to complain about the prayer and Bible reading students did in school. There was enough religious homogeneity that people could act as if a consensus existed, disregarding the rules of civility that apply in more pluralistic settings and giving the region its appearance of pervasive religiosity. (1990, 55)

If the Second Great Awakening resulted in an expansion of American evangelicalism to southern states, and the South's defeat in the Civil War led to an intensification of the evangelical tradition tied inseparably to southern culture, then the fundamentalist-modernist controversy likewise played a role. From about 1920 until after World War II, it marginalized evangelicalism everywhere except in the old Confederacy.

The Fundamentalist-Modernist Controversy
and Southern Religion

Throughout most of the nineteenth century, the term *evangelical* was more or less synonymous with *Protestant*. Not until the closing decades of that century did Protestants in America begin to align themselves along theologically liberal and conservative lines, a distinction that blurred even denominational boundaries. Liberal Protestants tried to reconcile their religious beliefs with new insights about the nature of reality from the natural and social sciences, while conservatives resisted the progress being made in scientific and humanistic disciplines because it threatened the authority of their biblical faith and thus their way of life. This gradual but steady division in Protestant culture began in the late nineteenth century and blew wide open in the fundamentalist-modernist controversy of the 1920s, which solidified two distinct groups of Protestants—evangelicals and liberals. The former emphasized personal piety and salvation out of this world. The latter opened itself to the modern social order and concern for the fate of human beings in this world; theirs was a "public" rather than "private" faith. Over time, liberals abandoned the revivalistic methods of the nineteenth century designed to save individual souls and emphasized instead a "social gospel" that appropriated modern social theories for the transformation of the world as a whole (Stone 1991, 85–90; Marsden 1980).

The term *fundamentalist* was adopted in the 1920s to describe conservative Protestants who were loyal to the "fundamentals of the faith" and committed to battling liberalism in the churches and secularism in society at large. The fundamentalist crusade against modernism, peaking between 1910 and 1930, was fought over essentially two things: the evolutionary teachings of Darwin in the public schools and the increasing liberalism of the "mainline" churches, exemplified by the preaching of Harry Emerson Fosdick (Stone 1991, 90; Furniss 1954).

Symbolically, the central event of the fundamentalist-modernist controversy was the Scopes Trial in Dayton, Tennessee, in 1925. John T. Scopes, a high school science teacher, was arrested for teaching about Darwin's theories in a public school. With the backing of the American Civil Liberties Union and representation by the famous trial lawyer Clarence Darrow, Scopes unsuccessfully challenged Tennessee's anti-evolution statute, but the trial severely undermined the fundamentalist cause. Conservative Protestants saw it as an opportunity to squelch anti-Christian opposition to the faith. With the whole nation watching, William Jennings Bryan took it upon himself to defend the fundamentals of Christianity but was not up to Darrow's rigorous cross-examination, which challenged biblical authority. Bryan's answers appeared foolish, and fundamentalism was in the end discredited (Stone 1991, 90–95).

The defeat of fundamentalism signaled a historic shift in American Protestantism. Whereas fifty years earlier evangelicalism had been at the center of American culture, by the 1930s it had moved to the periphery, displaced by scientific modernism and religious liberalism. "Fundamentalism," writes George Marsden, "emerged from an era in which American evangelicalism was so influential that it was virtually a religious establishment; eventually, however, fundamentalism took on the role of a beleaguered minority with strong sectarian or separatist tendencies" (1980, 6–7). Region marked a fundamental social cleavage in this theological controversy. Evangelical Protestantism, having failed to assert its authority in a public arena, was marginalized everywhere but in the South. What had been taken for granted in nineteenth-century American culture was no longer received wisdom in the twentieth century.

The South's peripheral standing in American culture—its poverty, its rural population base, the Civil War defeat, and related factors—conspired to insulate Southerners from the corrosive effects of the new intellectual currents and social changes that threatened religious authority. But more importantly, because evangelicalism was by then part of the very fabric of southern life—evangelical piety and conventional morality being synonymous—the challenge to fundamentalism by northern intellectuals in the opening decades of the twentieth century was another attack on the integrity of southern culture, turning the South further inward and intensifying southern religion by forcing it into a defensive posture. Not merely Christian doctrine but the southern way of life was being challenged.

The effect of this challenge to fundamentalism was to solidify and intensify religious homogeneity in the South and to undermine and disestablish evangelicalism in the North. An understanding of these regional differences, still largely intact, is critical for interpreting the meaning of resurgent evangelicalism today. But first it is necessary to demonstrate the empirical basis for continuing to describe the South as an evangelical subculture.

The Religious Geography of the American South

Religious geographers have in recent decades developed several classifications of America's religious regions using a variety of statistical methods. Notably, however, they reach quite similar conclusions regarding the major religious regions. This is especially true with respect to the South. For instance, Wilber Zelinsky (1961), using church membership data from 1952 and starting from the premise that the conventionally identified regions of the country are culturally as well as politically and economically distinctive, portrays the South as a religious region dominated by two denominational groups: Baptists and Methodists. James R. Shortridge (1977), using 1971 church membership data, identifies a configuration of conservative Protestantism in the deep South by using a procedure that sorts liberal and conservative Protestant groups. William M. Newman and Peter L. Halvorson (1982), using the same data used by Shortridge, develop a scheme that specifies a grouping of "southern Anglo-Calvinists," which overlaps geographically and denominationally with the Zelinsky and Shortridge typologies.

By all accounts, the South as a religious region is one in which Baptists are dominant, Methodists are plentiful, and Presbyterians are also well represented. These three church bodies are the evangelical establishment in the South; their missionary work during the late eighteenth and early nineteenth centuries introduced and popularized the evangelical style of Christian worship that still dominates the region. Even though time and historical circumstance are eroding evangelicalism's orthodox edge and sectarian offshoots of these major religious organizations have grown into large and influential denominations, the South in the latter half of the twentieth century remains steadfastly evangelical, according to aggregate church membership data. If there is any doubt that the region's evangelical core is still intact, it need only be observed that virtually all the nationally prominent televangelists of the last decade broadcast from somewhere south of the Mason-Dixon line. This hegemony is in stark contrast with the diversity of religious life in the rest of the country.

One way to describe these regional differences is to speak of religious establishment and disestablishment not in formal legal terms but in cultural terms. The evangelical faith is still normative in the South but not outside the South. Several findings from Phillip E. Hammond's study (1992; see especially chapter 6) of religious disestablishment in the United States deepen and reinforce this portrait of regional differences. Using individual-level survey data from four states, which serve as regional surrogates, Hammond makes the following observations.

(1) Ninety-four percent of North Carolinians claim a religious preference, three-fourths of whom are "conservative Protestant," a category roughly equivalent to my use of the term *evangelical*. That tradition dominates the cultural landscape in the South like no religion anywhere else in the country.

(2) By contrast, 82 percent of the people in Massachusetts claim a religious preference, but only 15 percent are conservative Protestant. Somewhat more than half (58 percent) are Roman Catholic. In California, a

fifth of the population has no religious preference. Among those who have a preference, no one religious tradition commands the allegiance of more than a third (32 percent conservative Protestant, 31 percent Roman Catholic). California is an especially pluralistic culture.

(3) People in North Carolina are more involved in parish life, more pious in practice, more orthodox in belief, and attach greater social importance to their religious commitments than do people in Massachusetts, Ohio, or California.

(4) Conservative Protestants more successfully retain their young people than do other Protestants in this country. Eighty-four percent of those reared conservative Protestant are still in the fold, compared to 60 percent among moderates and 58 percent among liberals. But what is often not appreciated is that the pull of tradition is much stronger in the South. The figures for conservative Protestants by region are as follows: a 93 percent retention rate in North Carolina, 82 percent in Ohio, 71 percent in California, and 63 percent in Massachusetts.

In short, evangelical culture still reigns in the South, while evangelical churches outside the South, by contrast, are culturally marginal. At best they must operate in an open and highly competitive religious market. That is the pluralistic context that southern churches do not face, but it is what they move into when they leave the South. This has enormous consequences for interpreting resurgent evangelicalism.

Finally, what about religious diversity *within* the South? Much has been made of the predominance of evangelicalism in the South—its Bible Belt mystique—but as the study of southern religion has matured over the last twenty years, more attention has been given to the region's religious diversity. Harrell's *Varieties of Southern Evangelicalism* (1981) exemplifies this turn, as does Hill's *Varieties of Southern Religious Experience* (1988). The essays in these two volumes remind us that there are Catholics and Jews in the South, that fundamentalists and evangelicals are not the same theologically or culturally, that there are differences between Holiness and Pentecostal churches, and that the experiences of black and white evangelicals in the South are worlds apart. Despite this rich variation, however, the existence of an identifiably southern style of religiousness is undeniable.

Three caveats are in order before I turn to definitional issues. First, I am not arguing that southern religion is monolithic. A Southern Baptist preacher interviewed for this study quipped that there are as many different churches in the South as there are Baptists, but, indeed, most are Baptist. Given the dominant role of evangelicalism in southern history, therefore, it makes sense to talk about "southern-style religion" as a unitary force, particularly since my agenda is to examine the consequences of regional differences in American religion and culture.

Second, I am not suggesting that evangelical Protestantism is unique to the South or implying that there are no vital evangelical communities elsewhere in America. That is patently false (for example, Billy Graham's headquarters are in Minneapolis). But nowhere else in America is this tradition found as a vigorous cultural force as it is in the South.

Finally, this study does not explore the rich history of evangelical Protestantism in African American communities. Rather I am interested in the resurgence of evangelicalism among "white" Americans because that is the demographic base for the new Christian right—the most visible and politically significant feature of resurgent evangelicalism. Groups like the Moral Majority in the 1980s and the Christian Coalition in the 1990s grew out of the culture of white-ethnic southerners. Therefore, this is a study of "white" evangelical Protestantism.

Defining Southern-Style Religion

The term *evangelical* has come to refer to the sector of American Protestantism that emphasizes the New Testament notion that God, through Jesus Christ, bestows a saving grace on human beings without regard to worthiness (in contrast to the theology of good works). As a consequence, evangelicals believe that a spiritual rebirth, acknowledging personal sinfulness and Christ's atonement, is essential for salvation. This process is referred to as a born-again experience. Most evangelicals also interpret the Bible literally, rejecting the critical and historical approaches to scripture adopted by so-called modernists in this century. Finally, evangelicals are committed to proselytizing—converting others to the Christian faith.[2] Some scholars of American religion distinguish evangelicals from fundamentalists, Pentecostals, and charismatics. Depending on the research agenda, these distinctions may be crucial. For this work they are not. I follow Randall Balmer's (1989) use of the word *evangelical* as an umbrella term to refer broadly to conservative Protestantism in America, including fundamentalists, Pentecostals, and charismatics but also including

---

2. In a sense, there is no "correct" definition of evangelicalism. The three characteristics I identify here—born-again experience, literal interpretation of scripture, and commitment to converting others—are the most basic and widely accepted definitional features of this wing of American Protestantism. For other discussions of definitional issues in studying evangelicalism, see R. Stephen Warner (1979), Nancy Tatom Ammerman (1982), and James Davison Hunter (1983).

others who, in rejecting those three labels, nonetheless answer to the term *evangelical*.

While I do not wish to distinguish among evangelicals on theological grounds, I am arguing that the history of religion in the American South has preserved and remade a variety of Protestantism not found in other regions of the country throughout most of this century. Southern religion is a form of evangelical Protestantism that has come to be distinctive in the following ways: (1) it is an emotional, revivalistic form of Christian worship, historically exemplified by camp-meetings and still present in southern culture today, though in a modified form; (2) it has a sectarian character, exemplified by the plethora of fiercely independent church bodies that have sprung up on southern soil over the last 175 years; (3) it demands that its adherents live righteously, displaying popular southern piety; and (4) it is associated with the culture of white southerners—in other words, a part of southern identity.

Is southern evangelicalism different from other forms of evangelicalism? As conventionally defined, southern-style religion is essentially what we have come to understand contemporary evangelicalism to be. Donald G. Mathews, for example, writes of religion in the Old South that "the Christian life is essentially a personal relationship with God in Christ, established through the direct action of the Holy Spirit, an action which elicits in the believer a profoundly emotional conversion experience. This existential crisis, the *New Birth* as Evangelicals called it, ushers the convert into a life of holiness characterized by religious devotion, moral discipline, and missionary zeal" (1977, xvi). Compare this to the following definition of contemporary American evangelicalism as offered by Martin Marty:

> By evangelical, I mean a Jesus-centered form of Protestantism that emerged during the last quarter millennium largely on Anglo-American soil. It is generated through the call for a turning from the old self and world, in a conversion through an intense experience of Jesus Christ by the power of the Holy Spirit. This conversion it reinforces with a fresh resort to biblical authority supported by high claims for the literal accuracy of the Bible. Evangelicalism then issues in a plea for ordered moral behavior and efforts to witness to and share the faith in the form of evangelicalism. (1981, 9)

What is the relationship between southern-style religion and evangelical Protestantism generally? I argue that contemporary, resurgent evangelicalism is similar to old-time southern religion precisely because its roots lie in the South.

While evangelical Protestantism did not originate in the South, for specific historical reasons it has come to be identified with southern culture, and the South is the only region of the country where evangelicalism has remained a powerful cultural force in this century. Thus it is a kind of cultural repository for the evangelical tradition and the appropriate place to look to begin to understand the recent resurgence of born-again Christianity outside the South. Anecdotal evidence suggests that southern religion, like southern culture generally, is moving into mainstream American society, and there is some empirical basis for such a claim.

CHAPTER TWO

Resurgent Evangelicalism
and the Spread of Southern Religion

The "country and westernization" of American culture has
found its religious counterpart in the northward seepage of
evangelical styles. Southerners, including the new Sunbelt
arrivals, need to know the evangelical past to understand
themselves and their neighbors. The rest of America, Canada,
and Western Europe have to learn more in order to come to
terms with their upstart neighbor in the American South.
For if anywhere in the modern world religion and culture are
bonded—whether on bleak dusty hilltops in remote reaches
of Texas or in downtowns of the Dallases—it is in the Sunbelt.
. . . The new prosperous Evangelicalism did not just appear
out of nowhere. It has roots that are tangled with many other
subterranean forces. It has branches that entwine with non-
religious branches under the Southern sky.

Martin Marty

Whatever else churches are, they are social institutions and subject to
change. A religious tradition dominant in one historical period may lose currency in another—or regain it. *How* that change happens is a sociological question. Following the southernization thesis advanced by Egerton, I believe that
resurgent evangelicalism is partly explained by the growth of southern religion
outside the South; or, more precisely, evangelicalism's new nationwide vitality
is a function of the dispersion of southern evangelicals. As one cultural geogra-
pher put it, "wherever there are Southern Baptists there is southern culture"
(Gastil 1975, 53).

Based on an analysis of church membership trends and interregional migration patterns, I argue that southern churches outside the South (Southern
Baptist and Assemblies of God, for example) grew faster in the 1970s and 1980s

than old-line evangelical churches whose historical and geographic base is not southern (such as the Lutheran Church Missouri Synod, Seventh-Day Adventists, and Church of the Nazarene); and furthermore, southern churches grew fastest in regions with especially high concentrations of southern migrants. Data supporting these claims are presented in the following pages.

Church Membership Data—Strengths and Limitations

The data for this analysis come from the three most comprehensive church membership studies now available, published by the Glenmary Research Center (Johnson, Picard, and Quinn 1974; Quinn et al. 1982; Bradley et al. 1992). These data were compiled at the county level for all major religious denominations for three time periods, 1971, 1980 and 1990, thus permitting an examination of church membership change over time. Comparable membership data from these three studies are available for fifty denominations. To ease recoding and classification, and to minimize the effect of reporting errors by smaller church groups, only large denominations (those reporting at least 150,000 members) were included. Therefore, twenty of fifty potentially usable denominations have been excluded from the analysis (see appendix A). However, they represent only 2 percent of the total church membership in all fifty denominations. In other words, the thirty denominations I use contain the other 98 percent. Hence those excluded do not substantially affect the analysis.

While these membership data are the best available, they are problematic in some respects. The most critical issue is that no standardized definition of church membership was employed. Since there is no generally accepted statistical definition of church membership, the designation of members rested finally with the denominations themselves. It can safely be assumed, however, that these definitions did not change within denominations from year to year. A second ambiguity is that since not all churches reported the number of "adherents" (regular attenders) but reported instead only the smaller number of official members, estimates for this larger category were generated through a standardized formula based on the number of "communicants" (official members). This analysis uses the broader of these two categories, an estimate by religious organizations of how many people are regular attenders. A third ambiguity is that membership statistics are reported for the county in which the church itself is located, not the county in which the member resides, though in most cases the county of residence corresponds to the county where the church is located. Finally, there is the issue of the accuracy of reporting. Recent research (Hadaway, Marler, and Chaves 1993) suggests that poll data overestimate the number of church attenders in the United States, and social scientists have for some time suspected that denominationally generated data inflate affiliation rates as mainline churches in particular are slow to clean their membership rolls in an era of decline (Hoge and Roozen 1979). Self-reported data in the Glenmary studies may therefore overstate church membership in the United States, but the bias is probably consistent and will not affect the analysis of change over time or the difference between denominations. Most large denominations maintain national offices that routinely receive statistical reports from their individual congregations; data for these denominations are therefore fairly reliable. Smaller denominations and denominations that allow local churches a great deal of autonomy, on the other hand, provide less complete data, but most of those are among the omitted denominations.

Despite these ambiguities, these religion data are the best census-like information available on membership in major religious denominations in America. Moreover, they are compatible in time with United States census periods so that church membership data can be correlated with population and migration data. Third, county-level data are collapsible and allow for an analysis of membership trends at a variety of levels, including state and region. Finally, these data are valuable because they span the 1970s and '80s, a crucial period for understanding evangelical resurgence because it is when conservative Protestants gained new visibility.

Classification of Protestant Denominations

How do I operationalize "southern-style religion"? Because southern religion is essentially evangelical in character, I begin by distinguishing between "mainline" and "evangelical" denominations. These categories are not unlike the distinction between liberal plus moderate (my "mainline") and conservative (my "evangelical") made by others studying religious change in American society (see Kelley 1972; Roof and McKinney 1987). Two criteria have been used to distinguish between southern and nonsouthern evangelicals. First, did a given denomination originate in the South, and/or do the majority of its members currently reside there? Second, can a given denomination be said to be historically a "people's" church (folk religion) as opposed to an "establishment" church? Affirmative answers to *both* of these questions mean that a given denomination is classified as southern evangelical. Denominations that cannot answer both of these questions affirmatively are classified as nonsouthern evangelical. The results of this classification scheme are reported in detail in appendix B.

Few scholars will disagree with the classification here of southern evangelical denominations, but the nonsouthern category is problematic because it is residual. Denominations in this group are clearly not mainline, nor can they be called southern evangelical by the criteria employed here. Moreover, there is considerable heterogeneity within the group. One might argue, for instance, against splitting the Church of God in Anderson, Indiana (nonsouthern), and the Church of God in Cleveland, Tennessee (southern), but whereas three-fourths of all Cleveland members reside in the South, only one-third of the Anderson members do so. Geographically, the Anderson church is not a southern denomination. Other nonsouthern groups that are stylistically similar to southern denominations include Church of the Nazarene, International Church of the Foursquare Gospel, Free Methodists, and Christian Churches and Churches of Christ. (This latter group is not to be confused with the Churches of Christ, which is clearly southern but for which data are unavailable for 1971.) The proportion of church membership located in the South for each of these four denominations is 32 percent, 9 percent, 10 percent, and 32 percent respectively.

The southern branches of the Presbyterian and Methodist churches pose another problem. Both were among the evangelical vanguard in the nineteenth century, yet I do not count them here as southern evangelical. To be sure, the southern Presbyterian Church U.S. (which merged with the northern branch in 1983) is decidedly southern and conservative, but in the twentieth century it has not exhibited the populist and regional character of the Baptist and other southern evangelical groups. Southern Methodists fall somewhere between Baptists and Presbyterian as prototypical southern evangelicals and are therefore useable, but the Glenmary data report membership only for the United Methodist Church, thus not allowing for a separate treatment of the northern and southern branches of Methodism.

While there may be other fruitful ways of classifying the denominations in this study's residual category, they at least have in common the fact that none is geographically southern.

Which Churches Are Growing Where?

Studies of church membership trends in the United States over the last two decades show that evangelical churches are growing while churches on the liberal wing are in decline. My findings are consistent with that pattern. Table 2.1 shows that the number of evangelicals grew by almost 13 percent during the 1970s, compared with a membership loss of more than 3 percent in the Protestant mainline.[1] That pattern held in the 1980s; evangelicals grew by

---

1. "Church membership" refers to the total number of "adherents"—a broad, inclusive category that in the Glenmary studies means "all members, including full members, their children and the estimated number of other regular participants who are not considered as communicant, confirmed or full members" (Quinn et al. 1982, xiii).

about 12 percent while the mainline decline accelerated (-5.4 percent). By comparison, the population of the United States as a whole grew by about 9 percent per decade. Between 1971 and 1990 evangelical churches added 6.1 million members to their rolls; liberal and moderate Protestants lost 2.6 million devotees. The net effect is that more people now attend evangelical churches in this country than affiliate with congregations in the old Protestant mainline. However, the relative strength and shifting fortunes of these Protestant groups vary significantly by region of the country.

TABLE 2.1

Number of Church Adherents Nationwide, Evangelical Compared to Mainline Protestant, 1971–1990 (in millions)

Protestant Type	1971	1980	1990	Change In 1970s	Change In 1980s	Total Change (1971–1990)
Evangelical	23.5	26.5	29.6	+3.0 (+12.9%)	+3.1 (+11.7%)	+6.1 (+26.0%)
Mainline	30.6	29.6	28.0	−1.0 (−3.3%)	−1.6 (−5.4%)	−2.6 (−8.5%)
U.S. Population	207.5	227.0	248.7	+19.5 (+9.4%)	+21.7 (+8.7%)	+41.2 (+19.9%)

Given the religious history of the former Confederacy, it is no surprise that two-thirds of all evangelicals in the United States reside in the South; nor is it surprising that evangelicalism shows a healthy rate of growth in the South. What is remarkable is that evangelical churches are growing in regions where conservative Protestantism has not fared well in this century (see Table 2.2). Evangelicals in the West, for example, grew by 45 percent between 1971 and 1990, a higher rate of growth than in the South (30 percent), and they are growing in the North as well. By comparison, mainline Protestantism is relatively strong in the South and in uniform decline elsewhere. Together these patterns suggest that the geographic spread of religious styles in America may have a reciprocal quality: conservative Protestantism is growing outside the South (the process I'm calling the southernization of American religion) while liberal and moderate Protestantism is growing inside the South (a process that can be called Americanization).

TABLE 2.2

Percent Change in the Number of Protestant Church Adherents, Evangelical vs. Mainline, by Region, 1971–1990

Region	Protestant Type	
	Evangelical	Mainline
South	+30.2 ($n=14,927$)*	+7.7 ($n=9,178$)
West	+45.5 ($n=2,296$)	−12.5 ($n=3,271$)
Northeast	+13.4 ($n=824$)	−16.1 ($n=6,884$)
Northcentral	+9.7 ($n=5,404$)	−16.1 ($n=11,258$)

*The Base-n, reported in thousands, is the number of adherents in 1971.

These findings are consistent with the southernization thesis, but if resurgent evangelicalism is essentially the spread of southern religion, then specifically southern evangelicals ought to be growing faster than nonsouthern evangelicals, and their growth should be greatest outside the southern states. The figures in Table 2.3 indicate that while both types of evangelicals grew in the 1970s, membership among southern evangelicals increased by more than 16 percent compared to an increase of less than 6 percent among nonsouthern evangelicals, and during the 1980s, only southern evangelicals added to their ranks (by 18 percent). Nonsouthern evangelicals lost about 4 percent of their membership. In absolute terms, southern evangelicals outnumber their nonsouthern counterparts 3 to 1, up from a 2 to 1 ratio in 1971. These church membership data show that resurgent evangelicalism is indeed a function of the growth of southern religion. But it is not a phenomenon confined to the South; southern evangelicals are multiplying in all regions of the country, and thus they are changing America's religious landscape.

Table 2.4 shows the regional distribution and growth rates of southern as compared to nonsouthern evangelicals. While southern evangelical churches are concentrated in the South (more than 80 percent) and grew by almost one-third in that region, they gained almost 2 million new adherents outside the South between 1971 and 1990. Moreover, their rate of growth during that

TABLE 2.3

Number of Evangelical Church Adherents, by Evangelical Type, 1971–1990 (in millions)

Evangelical Type	1971	1980	1990	Change 1971–1980	Change 1980–1990	Total Change
Southern	16.2	18.8	22.2	+2.6 (+16.1%)	+3.4 (+18.1%)	+6.0 (+37.0%)
Nonsouthern	7.3	7.7	7.4	+0.4 (+5.9)	−0.3 (−3.9%)	+0.1 (+1.4%)

period was impressive in all regions of the country (175 percent in the Northeast, 89 percent in the West, and 51 percent in the north central region). Conversely, nonsouthern evangelicals, while losing members in the Northeast and the north central states, increased their ranks in the South by 19 percent—a quarter-million new members. Again, there appears to be a reciprocal quality in the growth of Protestant traditions in non-native regions of the country.

TABLE 2.4

Percent Change in the Number of Southern vs. Nonsouthern Evangelical Church Adherents, by Region, 1971–1990

Region	Evangelical Type	
	Southern	Nonsouthern
South	+31.3 ($n=13,606$)*	+18.7 ($n=1,322$)
West	+88.7 ($n=934$)	+15.8 ($n=1,364$)
Northeast	+174.5 ($n=141$)	−20.1 ($n=683$)
Northcentral	+51.3 ($n=1,473$)	−5.9 ($n=3,931$)

*The Base-n, reported in thousands, is the number of adherents in 1971.

These findings make clear that southern religion, in particular, is on the rise nationwide. But is it keeping pace with population growth? In other words, is there any evidence that proportionately more Americans are expressing themselves in evangelical—and specifically southern—terms than before? Table 2.5 reports evangelical growth as a percent of the population by region of the country. The main story here is that while mainline Protestants and nonsouthern evangelicals are losing market share, southern religion is gaining ground in all regions of the country except the South, a finding reflected in the highlighted figures in the far right column in Table 2.5.[2]

TABLE 2.5

Church Adherents as a Percentage of the Population, by Region and Protestant Type, 1971–1990

Region	Protestant Type	1971	1980	1990	Change 1971–1990
South	South Evangel	21.50	20.68	20.91	−0.59
	Nonsouth Evangel	2.09	2.08	1.88	−0.21
	Mainline	14.51	13.33	11.56	−2.95
Northeast	South Evangel	0.28	0.51	0.76	+0.48
	Nonsouth Evangel	1.38	1.38	1.07	−0.31
	Mainline	13.90	13.15	11.37	−2.53
Northcentral	South Evangel	2.58	3.18	3.73	+1.15
	Nonsouth Evangel	6.89	6.78	6.20	−0.69
	Mainline	19.72	17.52	15.82	−3.90
West	South Evangel	2.62	3.03	3.33	+0.71
	Nonsouth Evangel	3.82	3.53	2.99	−0.83
	Mainline	9.17	6.87	5.42	−3.75

Table 2.6 shows membership change in southern evangelical churches as a percent of the population by nonsouthern census divisions, and Table 2.7 shows the same data by state. According to these data, southern evangelicalism is gaining market share in all but two states (Alaska and New Mexico). Not sur-

---

2. These figures are conservative and would be more dramatic if our data included membership in independent evangelical churches, an increasingly popular form of conservative Protestantism. In fact, sectarianism is a characteristic feature of southern religion, and more independent— "community"—churches with an evangelical style have been founded over the last two decades than any other Protestant type (Hammond 1992). Unfortunately, because they are decentralized and nondenominational, no reliable data are available on membership growth in these churches.

TABLE 2.6

Membership Change in Southern Evangelical Churches as a Percentage of the Population, 1971–1990, Rank-Ordered by Marketshare Change

Rank	Census Division	1971	1980	1990	Change 1971–1990
1	West North Central	5.16	5.86	6.59	+1.43
2	East North Central	1.53	2.07	2.53	+0.99
3	Pacific West	2.11	2.60	2.82	+0.72
4	Mountain West	4.21	4.24	4.82	+0.60
5	Middle Atlantic	0.30	0.54	0.80	+0.50
6	New England	0.24	0.40	0.66	+0.42

prisingly, north central states bordering the South—Missouri, Indiana, and Ohio—rank high on the list. Southern evangelicals in Missouri, for instance, were 14.7 percent of the population in 1971 and grew to 17.4 percent by 1990. The Northwest is the other region where southern evangelical growth as a percent of the population is notable. Wyoming, Montana, Washington, and Idaho are among the top ten states on the list (see Table 2.7), and Oregon ranks thirteenth.

TABLE 2.7

Membership Change in Southern Evangelical Churches as a Percentage of Population in Nonsouthern States, 1971–1990, Rank-Ordered by Marketshare Change

Rank	State	1971	1980	1990	Change 1971–1990
1	Missouri	14.70	16.19	17.44	+2.74
2	Wyoming	3.10	3.29	5.29	+2.19
3	Montana	1.89	2.54	3.59	+1.70
4	Kansas	3.71	4.34	5.17	+1.46
5	Indiana	1.83	2.55	3.21	+1.38
6	Washington	1.75	2.62	3.09	+1.34
7	Ohio	1.40	2.13	2.73	+1.33
8	Hawaii	2.00	2.20	3.23	+1.23
9	Idaho	2.01	2.45	3.01	+1.00
10	Illinois	2.46	2.89	3.42	+0.96
11	Nebraska	1.06	1.50	1.94	+0.88
12	North Dakota	1.44	1.76	2.31	+0.87
13	Oregon	2.02	2.88	2.84	+0.82

(continued on next page)

TABLE 2.7 (con't)

Membership Change in Southern Evangelical Churches as a Percentage of Population in Nonsouthern States, 1971–1990, Rank-Ordered by Marketshare Change

Rank	State	1971	1980	1990	Change 1971–1990
14	South Dakota	1.32	1.53	2.11	+0.79
15	Nevada	2.25	2.97	2.96	+0.71
16	Michigan	0.94	1.27	1.63	+0.69
17	Iowa	0.70	1.24	1.33	+0.63
18	Colorado	3.05	3.04	3.64	+0.59
19	Wisconsin	0.39	0.70	0.97	+0.58
20	Pennsylvania	0.38	0.70	0.95	+0.57
21	California	2.12	2.53	2.68	+0.56
22	Minnesota	0.50	0.68	1.05	+0.55
23	Connecticut	0.27	0.51	0.81	+0.54
24	Arizona	5.39	5.05	5.92	+0.53
25	New York	0.25	0.46	0.74	+0.49
26	Maine	0.39	0.57	0.81	+0.42
27	New Jersey	0.30	0.50	0.71	+0.41
28	Massachusetts	0.16	0.32	0.55	+0.39
29	New Hampshire	0.35	0.41	0.72	+0.37
30	Rhode Island	0.22	0.26	0.55	+0.33
31	Utah	0.91	0.91	1.22	+0.31
32	Vermont	0.47	0.43	0.64	+0.17
33	Alaska	7.38	6.43	7.24	−0.14
34	New Mexico	12.55	11.77	12.06	−0.49

It is also instructive to consider the ratio between mainline Protestants and southern evangelicals, whether or not it changed between 1971 and 1990 in a given region. That figure represents the relative strength of the two wings of Protestant presence in America. Table 2.8 presents the mainline/southern evangelical ratio for nonsouthern census divisions. In the Northeast, mainline Protestants outnumbered southern evangelicals almost 50 to 1 in 1971; at the end of the decade the ratio was down to 15 to 1. The ratios are much smaller in other regions (where there is greater balance between southern evangelicals and mainline Protestants), and parity is increasing.

Throughout this analysis I contrast evangelical Protestantism with main-line Protestantism. Evangelicals themselves find this distinction somewhat of-

TABLE 2.8

Change in the Ratio of Mainline Protestants to Southern Evangelicals, 1971–1990, Rank-Ordered by 1990 Ratios

Rank	Census Divisions	Ratio 1971	Ratio 1980	Ratio 1990
1	New England	49.93	26.61	14.07
2	Middle Atlantic	48.53	25.77	15.15
3	East North Central	11.00	7.15	5.19
4	West North Central	5.18	4.11	3.37
5	Pacific West	4.08	2.46	1.76
6	Mountain West	2.60	1.92	1.40

fensive (it locates them on the fringe of American culture) and argue that mainline churches are more appropriately referred to as liberal Protestant. Scholars of American religious life adopted the term *mainline* because it described something about the fit between liberal-moderate Protestantism and American culture more generally. For most of the twentieth century they were comfortable together, while evangelicals were a marginal group. A religion's proximity to the core values of a culture is a useful distinction, of course, but only if it changes to reflect shifting fortunes.

The data presented here show the numerical superiority of evangelical groups in America. Evangelicalism's new popularity and its fit with the conservative mood of American civic life in the 1980s and 1990s suggest that perhaps conservative Protestant groups are becoming the new mainline. Certainly their numeric strength today and their expanded geographic presence warrant a reassessment of their social status in American life, but whether or not it makes sense to speak of evangelicalism as the new Protestant mainline depends on whether or not it reflects values held in the wider culture, an issue addressed in later parts of this book.

Most of the growth of evangelicalism during the 1970s and 1980s is accounted for by increased membership in southern evangelical churches in particular. The evidence thus far supports the argument that the spread of southern religion is a source of the nationwide resurgence of evangelicalism, but *how* is this happening?

There are two possibilities: southern churches in places like the West Coast and New England are drawing from a population of displaced southerners— those familiar with the culture—or they are successfully attracting nonsoutherners. Perhaps migrants from the South carry on their religious traditions in a new location; perhaps southern religion is appealing to a new population base. One or both propositions must be true.

Southernization and Migration

In their book *American Mainline Religion*, Wade Clark Roof and William McKinney observe that many conservative Protestants

> migrated out of the South after World War II and settled in towns and cities, often in the Midwest and Northeast. They have carried with them their transplanted "southern-style" faiths. Regional movement of this kind . . . no doubt helps explain the emergence of a broader national base for evangelicalism and fundamentalism. These faiths have long been sustained by traditions deeply rooted in the American South, and they continue so today through the cultural diaspora of southerners into the other regions of the country. (1987, 134)

However plausible this idea that culture travels as people travel, Roof and McKinney offer no conclusive evidence that the spread of southern culture is related to the movement of southerners. But there are good reasons to consider the migration thesis. It is well known that the population of the United States is increasingly mobile. People rarely stay as adults in the communities where they were raised, and while they most often move for economic or other reasons—new opportunities, new challenges—people carry their culture with them in some form, leading at least to the possibility of social change. If southerners are moving out of the South, it is not unreasonable to expect them to display their southernness in a new location. And in fact, the historical record shows that this has happened.

The Appalachian "hillbillies" moved to northern cities during World War II and were transformed by the experience, but they did not abandon their cultural heritage overnight. As they moved, the South—their particular version of it—moved with them. Likewise, the Dust Bowl migration from Arkansas, Oklahoma, and Texas in the 1930s depopulated the plains states but populated California and, to a lesser extent, the Pacific Northwest. To this day cities like Bakersfield in the San Joaquin Valley reflect these southern roots in country music and old-time religion, among other things.

The extent of southern culture in California can be seen on a blue-highway drive between Death Valley and Bakersfield. The small towns that populate that territory have more churches than banks, gas stations, and grocery stores combined, and their names are telling: Church of the Fire Baptized,

Church of the Open-Bible, Pentecostal Holiness, Church of Christ, Independent Baptist, and so on. All are evangelical, sectarian, and very southern, at least in origin.

Gary Bouma demonstrates the plausibility of a diffusion model for explaining religious change. He criticizes Dean Kelley's (1972) argument that the Christian Reformed Church (CRC) grew faster than the closely related Reformed Church in American (RCA) because it was doctrinally more conservative. Bouma shows that "the greater growth of the CRC is best explained by patterns of Dutch immigration after World War II and higher CRC fertility rates, but not by the appeal of the CRC to those not already members" (1979, 127). In this case, demography—particularly migration—goes further than the appeal of religious doctrine in explaining church growth. The important point is that the CRC grew because it drew on a population of culturally like-minded people. Similarly, I argue that southern religion is growing because it attracts displaced southerners.

The connection between migration and religious change has received little scholarly attention. The work of Roger Stump (1984), however, provides one exception. His concern is whether religious commitment (frequency of church attendance and strength of identification) among migrants will rise or fall depending on the norms of religious behavior in the regions to which they move. My concern, too, is whether migrants adapt to their new surroundings, but my variable is denominational switching rather than strength of commitment. When southerners move, in other words, do they look for (or establish) a Southern Baptist church, or do they attend whatever church is conveniently located in their new community? Stump found that being uprooted, rather than necessarily weakening religious commitment, leads to increased commitment among migrants to regions of higher native commitment, such as the South. But the reverse is also true; migrants to the West show lower levels of commitment than people in their regions of origin. His conclusion is that migration, contrary to expectations, may not be eroding regional religious differences in the United States. My contention is that regional religious differences are diminishing not because movers have become uniformly less religious (Stump's null hypothesis) but rather because certain people who move a great deal, namely southerners, carry with them particularly strong—and conservative—religious traditions, thus spurring the revitalization of evangelicalism, a process aptly characterized as the southernization of American religion.

What is the evidence that the spread of southern religion is related to the migration of southerners? Table 2.9 reports southern evangelical growth compared to in-migration from the South for six nonsouthern regions of the country (census divisions). It happens that there are more new southern evangelicals

TABLE 2.9

Relationship Between Southern Evangelical Growth and In-Migration from the South, 1971–1990 (nonsouthern census divisions only)

Census Division	Migrants from the South	So. Evangelical Growth, 1971–1990	Ratio Mig:SEG
New England	433,944	58,080	7:1
Middle Atlantic	1,065,489	188,209	6:1
East North Central	1,560,749	441,135	4:1
West North Central	714,213	313,410	2:1
Mountain West	824,267	294,215	3:1
Pacific West	1,494,988	530,801	3:1

on the Pacific coast than anywhere else, a count that reflects the large number of new adherents in California. The east north central states (Illinois, Indiana, and Ohio) show the second-highest number of new adherents. While southern evangelicals are growing at the highest rate in the Northeast, there were very few there to begin with; hence the absolute number of new adherents is relatively low. All these regions, nevertheless, experienced in-migration from the South at a rate that far exceeds the number of new southern evangelical adherents. In other words, it is possible that every new member in a southern evangelical church outside the South during the 1970s and '80s is a southerner in origin. Yet not every southerner who migrates affiliates with a southern church; in fact, a majority do not. Table 2.9 reports the ratio of southern migrants to new southern evangelicals for each region; they range from 2–1 to 7–1. The most remarkable feature of this table is the covariability of southern evangelical growth and southern migration. As the number of in-migrants from the South increases, so does the number of new southern evangelicals. The Pacific coast and east north central states have the highest number of new church affiliates and also the highest number of new southerners, for example.

A state-level analysis sharpens this pattern. In Table 2.10, migration and southern evangelical growth figures are presented in rank order for each nonsouthern state. California has the largest population of southern migrants of any state outside the South, and there are more new members in southern churches in California than in any other state. Ohio ranks second in migration

TABLE 2.10

Southern Evangelical Growth and In-Migration from the South, 1971–1990, Rank-Ordered by Number of Migrants

	Migration	Rank	Rank	Evangelical Growth
California	1,067,514	1	1	366,344
Ohio	495,870	2	3	145,704
Pennsylvania	421,667	3	10	66,930
New York	411,017	4	7	87,826
Illinois	381,983	5	5	115,509
Michigan	302,589	6	9	67,592
Missouri	277,425	7	2	157,460
Indiana	273,732	8	8	81,967
Colorado	251,413	9	12	49,806
New Jersey	232,805	10	15	33,453
Arizona	205,880	11	4	117,355
Washington	199,985	12	6	90,108
Kansas	176,974	13	13	44,946
Massachusetts	168,742	14	19	23,663
New Mexico	138,472	15	11	50,526
Connecticut	120,685	16	21	18,188
Wisconsin	106,575	17	16	30,363
Minnesota	95,089	18	17	26,919
Hawaii	93,463	19	20	19,735
Nevada	81,943	20	18	23,868
Oregon	77,196	21	14	37,194
Iowa	71,323	22	22	17,080
Utah	57,576	23	28	10,890
Alaska	56,830	24	25	15,188
Nebraska	56,183	25	26	14,674
Maine	48,992	26	29	6,010
New Hampshire	42,522	27	32	5,292
Idaho	35,294	28	23	15,478
Rhode Island	33,023	29	33	3,450
Wyoming	28,992	30	27	13,477
Montana	24,607	31	24	15,194
Vermont	19,980	32	34	1,477
North Dakota	19,158	33	31	5,701
South Dakota	18,061	34	30	5,792

from the South and third in church membership growth. Illinois is fifth on both lists. Vermont and the Dakotas rank at the bottom on both lists, and so on. In all cases, there are more new southerners in each state than new members in southern evangelical churches. This suggests that the growth of southern evangelicalism outside the South is in fact related to migration, a conclusion further supported by a county-level analysis of these data. Remarkably, there is a .80 correlation (Pearson's r, significant at $p=0.001$) between church membership growth and migration in the 1970s and a .72 correlation in the 1980s. A correlation of 1.0 indicates a perfect relationship. These findings suggest a strong link between resurgent evangelicalism in the 1970s and '80s and the diffusion of southerners to other regions of the country, but there are problems with this correlation.

Concluding that southern evangelical growth and migration from the South are related because they occur in the same geographic area constitutes an ecological correlation. In other words, it is possible that southern migrants chose not to affiliate with southern churches when they moved and that the growth of southern evangelicalism outside the South is attributable to its new popularity among nonsoutherners. There could be, for example, a high number of southern migrants into some California county and, simultaneously, a burst of new members in Assemblies of God churches, even though nonsoutherners fill the latter's pews on Sunday morning. Relating southern evangelical growth and out-South migration using county-level data is not making an individual-level correlation. Nevertheless, the possibility of drawing erroneous conclusions through an ecological correlation is minimized by increasing the number of area subdivisions in the analysis. That is, the validity of an ecological correlation is especially suspect when the unit of analysis is large, as with census regions or divisions, but the same correlation based on county-level data is more likely to match the underlying individual-level relationship (Robinson 1950). Although there are problems with this technique, my purpose is nonetheless served by showing that interregional migration is highly correlated with religious change; it is possible, though improbable, that resurgent evangelicalism and southern migration are not related, but it is also possible, and very probable, that they are related.

There is a second problem with explaining resurgent evangelicalism outside the South as a function merely of migration of people from the South. There are other components of a growth equation. Not only might growth in southern evangelical churches be accounted for by persons of nonsouthern origin, but also births and deaths affect growth rates. No data are available for these components of the growth equation, but it is known that evangelicals not only have higher birth rates but also retain their young more successfully than members of mainline churches (Hunter 1985, 153). Evangelical *growth*, therefore, is partly due to the addition of offspring. Yet that says nothing about the geographic spread of evangelicalism. Following Wilbur Zelinsky (1973, 77–79), I think population movement is especially important for understanding cultural change, and the westward migration of southerners has a rich history in the twentieth century.

The spread of southern evangelicalism observed in the 1970s and '80s really began during the depression and war years. The Dust Bowl migration brought large numbers of Baptists, Pentecostals, and other evangelicals out of Missouri, Arkansas, Oklahoma, and Texas into California. It was during those years that the Southern Baptist Convention broke its agreement with northern Baptists and began organizing state conventions outside the South for displaced southerners. Ammerman chronicles some of this migration history in *Baptist Battles*:

> During the Depression, Southerners had been leaving their homes in record number. Hundreds of thousands left behind desolate farms from Georgia to Oklahoma, traveling north and west in search of a better life. If they began looking for a church when they arrived in Ohio or California or Michigan they often found none to their liking. Churches that wore the name Baptist did not feel much like home to these Southern migrants. The Northern Baptist Churches usually offered a more formal style of worship and a more learned ministry than rural Southern Baptists had been used to. Few of the familiar hymns and none of the SBC programs were present, and Southerners strongly suspected that the people in these churches were too liberal for Southern tastes. . . . Soon enclaves of expatriates found each other and began to form congregations. Sometimes they labeled these churches "missionary" Baptist or "independent," [but] these were not disgruntled former Northern Baptists. These were people who went into a new territory and started Southern Baptist churches. (1990, 50–51)

In 1931, nineteen states in the union had a Southern Baptist Convention. Twenty-nine states had one in 1961, and today all fifty states do. Between 1941 and 1961, Southern Baptists grew from 5 million members and 25,000 churches to 10 million in over 32,000 churches, Ammerman reports (1990, 52–53). It is true that most religious bodies in America were expanding at that time, but the Southern Baptists outgrew everyone else and, along with Pentecostals, continued to grow during the 1970s and '80s, especially outside the South. Robert Wuthnow (1988, 186) reports that there were only 14 Southern Baptist churches outside the South at the start of World War II, but by 1960 there were nearly 700 hundred outside the South with a total membership of 175,000. My data show that in 1990 there were more than 7,300 churches and over 2.8 million Southern Baptists in nonsouthern states. Does culture really travel, as my interpretation of these data suggests?

The *Los Angeles Times* ran a story by Gerald Haslam on the Dust Bowl legacy in which it was reported that nearly one-eighth of the state of California now traces its ancestry to the migrants from Oklahoma and that the proportion is nearly one-half in the San Joaquin Valley. In that article, Haslam observes that the Central Valley "was not biscuit-and-gravy country before the Okies"; they brought it. He goes on to say that by "the second generation, those people are Californians, but the definition of what it means to be a Californian is changed by them [sic] having come here" (1989, 11). This is precisely my point. California and certain other regions were not evangelical country before the southern migrants came. They are now. For example, Kile Jim Yocum, a boy when his family made the trek from Oklahoma in search of economic opportunity, carried with him cultural baggage including faith preferences and denominational allegiance, Haslam reports. Today Yocum contributes $15,000 annually to the Church of Christ in Hanford, California—one of the largest distinctively southern church bodies in the country (38).

Resurgent evangelicalism can be understood as the spread of southern-style religion. This interpretation is supported by two facts: (1) among the expanding ranks of evangelicals, southern church bodies are growing at a higher rate than nonsouthern evangelical churches or the mainline more generally, especially outside the South; and (2) the growth of southern evangelicalism is related to an influx of southern migrants in nonsouthern regions of the country, particularly the Far West and Northeast. Taken together, these facts suggest that evangelicalism is on the rise nationwide because southerners carry their religious traditions with them when they leave the South and move elsewhere. The missionary history of southern church bodies and the migration patterns of southerners in the twentieth century support this thesis, but alone these results do not provide a definitive explanation of evangelical vitality in recent decades. My findings are consistent with the southernization thesis but not conclusive.

While it makes sense to characterize resurgent evangelicalism as a social process rooted, at least initially, in the migration of southerners, this periphery-to-center metaphor tells only part of the story. The geographic reshuffling of southerners explains the spread of southern religion, but not necessarily its growth in absolute terms. Are southern churches successfully recruiting nonsoutherners? And, if so, how "southern" are southern churches outside the South?

Answers to these questions are important for the following reason: if south-ern religion is growing around the country primarily by pulling in displaced southerners (or others reared in a conservative Protestant tradition), then its effect on the wider culture may be limited; that is, it will remain a migration-based subcultural phenomenon. On the other hand, if nonsouthern nonevangelicals are a large part of the current revival, then resurgent evangelicalism represents a deeper kind of cultural change, and it must be asked how and why nonevangelicals are coming into the evangelical fold. This ques-tion is explored in chapter 7. Meanwhile, it is useful to look at the results of field work in southern church settings outside the South to further investigate the southernization process and to assess the fit between southern churches and nonsouthern culture.

Part II

Southern Churches Outside the South

CHAPTER THREE

Preserving Fundamentalism
Portrait of a Struggling Baptist Church

Although there are now Southern Baptist churches in all
fifty states, 75 percent of the membership and the sources of
about 80 percent of the four billion dollars in annual financial contributions are concentrated still in the eleven states
of the Old Confederacy. The Convention has consistently
refused to change its name to anything less regional; the reasons for this have changed through time, but it has profound
cultural meaning. Every time Southern Baptists have made
this decision they have said something very important about
who they want to be as well as who they are.

Ellen M. Rosenberg

What do southern churches look like outside the South? Does it make
sense to refer to a Southern Baptist church in California as "southern religion"? Since these questions cannot be answered on the basis of quantitative
data, I spent six months doing field work in two southern churches in a midsize
California city, selecting the flagship congregations of the two largest southern
denominations included in the analysis in part 1, the Southern Baptist Convention and the Assemblies of God. The research involved participant observation in Sunday worship, formal and informal interviews with lay members
and staff, and participation in new members' classes (over six weeks) in both
congregations. My findings, reported in this chapter and the next, are start-
ling. Contrary to conventional wisdom and the southernization thesis, neither
California congregation is a hub of evangelical activity in the community; both
are struggling to survive.

Hope Baptist is a suburban rather than a downtown church, but it is nonetheless visible and accessible to the community in that it sits just off the main
boulevard connecting the city proper with a neighboring municipality. The
congregation moved to the present location in the late 1950s because it was

perceived to be a developing area in the community and thus fertile ground for church growth. Architecturally, Hope Baptist looks like an early 1960s suburban church (more horizontally than vertically expansive, with wood siding), lacking the stately character of the Episcopalian, Presbyterian, Congregational, and Methodist churches downtown, which are a century or more old. In a southern city, this Baptist congregation, affiliated with the Southern Baptist Convention, would be the "establishment" church, the magnificent red brick building at First and Main with a white steeple bell tower. In this California community it is not.

The rectangular sanctuary with its high ceiling seats perhaps 500 people. It has a traditional layout; long rows of pews are divided into three sections, a large center section and two side groups. It is rather modestly decorated. The windows have, rather than stained glass, panes of alternating soft colors. Nothing about them is ornate. The number of people attending worship averages about 150, roughly one-third of capacity. Remarkably, Hope Baptist is an ailing congregation. Its heyday has come and gone.

This Southern Baptist church in this central California city, consistent with the aggregate findings reported in part 1, grew steadily during the 1950s, '60s and '70s, but today it is struggling to survive. Hope Baptist is a "southern" church, continuous with the culture of the Old South in important ways, but it is no longer a center of evangelical vitality in this California community, as the southernization thesis would predict. The reasons for this are interesting.

Southern Baptists Outside the South

The history and current composition of Hope Baptist Church are illustrative of the southernization process described earlier. Like many Southern Baptist Convention churches, Hope Baptist started as a missionary effort, sponsored by a Southern Baptist congregation in a community thirty miles south and financially supported initially by the contributions of a single layman, a transplanted southerner. Founded in 1948, it was first called Trinity Baptist, and, while there is little record of the church's early history, there appears to have been a pattern of congregational conflict and instability coinciding with slow but steady growth. The following passage describing internal dissent at the founding of Trinity Baptist, taken from a denominational history of Southern Baptist churches in California, is vague but instructive:

> The history of the church has been somewhat tragic. In the first place the organization was hurried up in order to have . . . [the] executive secretary of the state convention present. [The] general missionary in the area, who had done much to develop the mission, was not advised

concerning plans to organize and was not present. The result was that some people got in the organization whose baptism was in question and who were suffering from doctrinal dyspepsia. Within a few months the church disbanded, leaving out of the new organization those who were regarded as objectionable.[1]

The comment about "objectionable" characters raises questions as to whether the turmoil was merely doctrinal and theological or was more cultural. Were the objectionable people southerners or persons reared outside the culture of the Old South and thus outsiders to Southern Baptist tradition? Were these early tensions reminiscent of the fundamentalist-modernist controversy of the 1920s, which many Southern Baptist churches initially avoided because of regional homogeneity? There is no written record by which to assess the religious and cultural meaning of these early struggles, but the turmoil is intriguing.

Trinity Baptist incorporated in 1950 but had divided by 1952. The splinter group, calling itself First Southern Baptist Church of Central Coast, was organized by former members of Trinity who were "dissatisfied with the pastoral leadership," church records note. One informant, one of the few remaining congregants old enough to have experienced the history firsthand, recalls that First Southern Baptist Church was more "progressive" on theological and moral issues; for instance, it was more open to allowing women to participate in leadership roles. This informant attended the splinter church for a time, but it folded in the mid-1960s, reportedly as a consequence of poor leadership. Meanwhile, the main body (then Trinity Baptist, now Hope Baptist) has been served by fourteen different pastors in forty-two years—on average, a new pastor every three years. The volatility in this congregation's history seems remarkable, though it did not prevent the church from growing.

Trinity Baptist benefited from its location in a suburban growth area during the 1960s and early '70s but since 1975 has been in steady decline. Membership figures are telling. Trinity Baptist had 61 members in 1954; it had 275 members in 1964. It built a new sanctuary in the early 1970s, and membership peaked at 750 in 1975. Now membership is less than 250, and worship typically involves between 100 and 150 parishioners, leaving many empty pews on Sunday morning. Somewhat contrary to findings presented in part 1, this pattern suggests that while resurgent evangelicalism was initially related to the spread of southern religion, southern churches today are not necessarily the center of evangelical vitality outside the South. That is true at least in this community.

---

1. This is reported in Looney (1954). No page numbers are given in the reference to protect the congregation's identity.

How did Trinity Baptist initially grow, and why is it in decline? More specifically, did it grow by drawing in southern migrants, and is its membership declining because it can no longer count on the ascriptive preferences related to regional identity? Put differently still, how southern is this congregation today, and is that relevant to understanding its growth and decline over time?

In the course of my visits to Hope Baptist Church, I met people from North Carolina, Mississippi, Arkansas, Oklahoma, and states such as Indiana that border southern states. I also met southerners only a generation removed from their homeland—people whose parents made the trek to California—and it is not uncommon in worship to hear the name of Jesus being praised with a thick southern accent or spot someone in Wrangler jeans and cowboy boots. No formal survey was made of the congregation, but perhaps only 3 in 10 parishioners I interviewed had any discernable direct ties to the South. Most of those interviewed, however, were reared in a conservative Protestant setting; they are evangelicals if not southerners by inheritance. But the congregation's southern ties are institutional as well as individual.

Hope Baptist is affiliated with the Southern Baptist Convention, and, while church leaders claim that the Baptist tradition of local church autonomy renders this relationship fairly meaningless, in fact their Convention affiliation structures the church in profound ways, both organizationally and culturally. Vince Taylor, one of Hope Baptist's two copastors, had this to say when questioned about the influence of the Southern Baptist Convention on local parish life: "Most churches don't give a rip about what the SBC is up to." The Convention, he says, is less a denomination than a loose association of churches that take little or no direction from national offices.

Yet linkages to the Southern Baptist tradition are everywhere apparent in Hope Baptist Church. For example, it was announced from the pulpit one Sunday that we were being joined that morning by several "brothers" (visiting pastors) from Arkansas. Another Sunday, representatives from the Southern Baptist General Convention of California participated in worship, apparently to shore up associational ties. The following week it was announced that a Baptist Student Union group (Baptist Student Union is the Convention's college campus ministry) from Mississippi would visit Hope Baptist in the summer to conduct a vacation Bible school for young people. That announcement was received enthusiastically by the congregation. Another Sunday we bade farewell to a couple in the church who were moving back to Missouri, their home state. The following month, Hope Baptist was to host the Central Coast Baptist Association meeting, a regional fellowship mid-level between the Southern Baptist state convention and the local congregation. In short, Hope Baptist's Southern Baptist Convention affiliation is no mere formality; it shapes and gives meaning to this congregation's life to such a degree that southerners out-side the South would find the religious culture familiar.

Ammerman describes this familiarity as it relates to the movement of southerners outside the South:

> [They] began to expect to find . . . Southern Baptist churches wherever they went. A vacationer could travel from coast to coast never missing a Sunday or Wednesday service in a Southern Baptist church. And, no matter where they were, the churches had a familiar feel of home. That comfortable feeling came in part from the Southern accents that might be heard; in part from the familiar biblical and evangelistic themes touched on in sermons and the warm, expressive character of the service; and in part it had to do with an assumption that because these people were Southern Baptist, they were brothers and sisters in the faith. Even as the regional base for family-feeling was disappearing, Southern Baptists still felt like a family. (1990, 59)

Hope Baptist is indeed that kind of home; it nurtures its historical roots not only by maintaining organizational ties to other Southern Baptist churches but also by preserving Southern Baptist culture locally, which is evident every Sunday in worship. What does this religious culture look like?

Southern Baptists may imagine themselves to be nonliturgical, but, as Ammerman reminds us, there is ritual among Southern Baptists as ordered as a Catholic Mass, and, like a Mass, it provides a universalizing experience for participants. She describes the routine of a Southern Baptist worship service as follows:

> The worship styles of SBC churches were in fact so routine that only the hymn numbers might change from Sunday to Sunday or place to place. Services varied mostly in the degree of polish and formality given to them in churches of varying sizes and resources. An organ . . . played familiar hymn tunes as the congregation gathered and again later as they dispersed. A period of congregational singing and prayers opened the service, followed by an offering (usually taken up by deacons). There was a special number from the choir or a soloist, a sermon of about thirty minutes, and an invitation hymn—often "Just As I Am" or "Softly and Tenderly"—when sinners were exhorted to be saved and new members were encouraged to join. Both sermon and invitation focused the atten-tion of listeners on the importance of making a personal decision to ac-cept Christ. The service closed with a spontaneous prayer from someone

in the congregation. Then everyone would file past the preacher at the door. (1990, 59–60)

This is exactly the order of worship I found in this SBC congregation in California. On February 23, 1992, for example, the worship service opened with an organ prelude followed by twenty minutes of hymns (including "How Great Thou Art" and "Great Is the Lord"), prayer and an offering, a New Testament reading, a thirty-minute "message" (a sermon entitled "A Place for You"), and an invitation (or altar call) that was accompanied by the hymn "Just as I Am." There was no spontaneous prayer to close the service, but the choir sang the benediction. This was a typical Sunday worship, and thus, by Ammerman's standard, Hope Baptist is undeniably Southern Baptist.

Ammerman also refers to the programs and SBC materials churches are likely to share, which traveling or relocated southerners can count on:

On Saturday night a traveler could read a Sunday school lesson for the next day, confident that the town's church would be studying the same lesson. The church's usher would hand out a Baptist Bulletin Service bulletin printed with a lovely inspirational color picture on the front and a story about the denomination's missionaries and other workers on the back. The hymnals in the pew racks would almost certainly be the official Baptist Hymnal, and the choir would probably sing a special number they had learned from *The Church Musician* (a Sunday School Board monthly) in robes they had ordered from their local Baptist Book Store. If the pastor had a college or seminary education, it was almost certainly from a Southern Baptist school. The church itself might have been designed by architects in Nashville, and it was perhaps financed with loans underwritten by the Home Mission Board. The visitor's card the traveler would fill out was probably printed by Convention Press (another Sunday School Board affiliate), and the church might be observing some special emphasis designated for this Sunday on the denominational calendar. (1990, 60)

Indeed, Hope Baptist's bulletins are printed by Baptist Bulletin Service, and material such as the March 22, 1992, insert to promote alcohol and drug abuse prevention is provided by the Christian Life Commission of the Southern Baptist Convention, headquartered in Nashville, Tennessee. The organizational ties between Hope Baptist Church and the SBC are substantial, therefore, but to whom do the SBC connection and the culture of southern evangelicalism appeal in this California community? Southern migrants played a critical role in the early history of "southern" churches outside the South, and that legacy is still apparent in this congregation, though southerners are no longer the majority. Emma Jean Beck, a longtime member of Hope Baptist, is one such person; she was born a Baptist and will die a Baptist.

Beck is perhaps sixty-five years old, single, formerly a public school music teacher, and a resident in the community for thirty-five years; but she came here from Oklahoma, where she was raised in a Southern Baptist church, and there is no way to explain her current affiliation apart from that history. She is a self-described liberal, perhaps the most liberal member of this congregation. She favors choice on abortion, for example, and is offended by traditional gender role segregation in church life and worship. As a trained musician, Beck is often asked to plan music programs for local and regional Baptist events, but because of the stipulation that a male will direct the music in her stead during worship, she routinely declines. According to Beck, the men in charge of worship argue that it is a sin for a woman to direct music in a church, that women should never be in a position of directing men. She finds that offensive in light of the Baptist tradition of freedom and tolerance. Yet she is an active and faithful member at Hope Baptist, and this is because it is the only SBC-affiliated church in the city. Given her moral and political views, her membership makes no sense otherwise. The power and durability of ascriptive cultural ties (region and religion) are thus doubly remarkable in Beck's case.

Beck is a Southern Baptist active at the regional and state level as well as in her local parish, though she is a maverick at Hope Baptist. Her relationship to the rest of the congregation, particularly the leadership, is reflective of larger liberal-conservative tensions in the Southern Baptist Convention. At Hope Baptist, as in the Convention as a whole, Beck's liberalism reflects the views of a minority—a small minority, but outside the South evangelical Protestantism and "traditional Christian morality" are not elements of the culture that are taken for granted, so she is comfortable with California's pluralism while most of her fellow parishioners are not. Beck may be a minority character in the church, but the church's repression of the kind of accommodation she represents may limit its appeal in the wider community.

There are, of course, other reasons people affiliate with a church. But people most often attend Hope Baptist for one or two simple reasons: They were raised in a Baptist church (or some similar conservative Protestant church) and thus are expressing ascriptive loyalties, as in Beck's case, and/or the church meets personal needs, whether they are physical, spiritual, social, or psychological; that is, it consoles and provides community for people cut loose from other social moorings (such as recent immigrants, the unemployed, and recent divorcees).

Bill and Lynn White are Beck's ideological opposite but belong to Hope Baptist for somewhat similar reasons; they are native North Carolinians and were reared Baptists. Yet there is more to the Whites' affiliation than ascriptive loyalties. Bill and Lynn are middle-class, in their mid-sixties, and recently retired. They attend Hope Baptist in part because the style of worship is familiar and therefore comfortable. During the new members' class (which the Whites are taking as a refresher course), the Whites appeared uninterested in the finer points of church doctrine, but they agreed with pastor Taylor's condemnations of homosexuality, abortion, and the general godlessness of the modern world, recurrent themes in this course designed to teach newcomers what it means to be a Baptist. However, there is more to the Whites' affiliation than their agreement with conservative cultural themes. Bill is a recovering alcoholic, and they credit Hope Baptist for his turnaround. The Whites lapsed from the church for many midlife years when career, family, and leisure activities took precedence. Only recently have they returned, a move motivated by Bill's efforts to deal with his alcoholism. They are once again faithful members of the congregation. Bill is chair of the Board of Deacons and a regular usher on Sunday morning. Lynn is active in women's circles. To the Whites, Hope Baptist Church is a caring and supportive community. They needed the church and are grateful for its exacting discipline as well as the fellowship they find in worship.

Finally, one of the most telling events in this church's recent history is its 1990 merger with Calvary Baptist Church, an affiliate of the Baptist Bible Fellowship (an ultraconservative, nonsouthern denomination). Calvary Baptist merged with Trinity Baptist to form Hope Baptist. Just before the merger, Trinity Baptist's membership had dropped below 50 (from 750 in 1975). Calvary Baptist had more than 200 members at the time of the merger. Calvary was the larger congregation, but Trinity had the facilities, so Calvary joined with Trinity. Their merger was prompted by organizational imperatives (Trinity's financial problems and Calvary's lack of facilities) but it was possible only because they shared a conservative ideology—fundamentalist Christianity and a moral agenda that embraces "traditional family values."

Two points about this event need to be made. First, the original SBC congregation declined by 93 percent between 1975 and 1990, before it was rescued by the merger. Thus, while Hope Baptist was part of resurgent evangelicalism through the 1970s, by 1990 it was on the verge of extinction. Second, these Southern Baptists did not survive by converting nonevangelicals; rather they brought in Christians of like mind. I witnessed only four baptisms in the church over a three-month period, and the only responses to the altar calls at the end of every Sunday service were reaffirmations of faith.

While this merged congregation remains a Southern Baptist affiliate, there have been struggles over the maintenance of SBC ties now that such a small proportion of congregants are southern in origin. Yet the leaders from both of the earlier congregations are committed to preserving the conservative moral culture that is characteristic of old-time southern religion, and this commitment may continue to hamper their growth in the long run.

Reasserting Identity in a Heterogeneous Culture

My assumption in this and subsequent chapters is that the relationship between church culture and surrounding culture is more important than organizational factors for understanding the vitality of "southern" churches outside the South. Hope Baptist is a *southern* Baptist church that affirmed its denominational allegiance by maintaining Southern Baptist Convention ties following the merger (despite the fact that Trinity was the smaller of the two merging congregations), and that reaffirmation of old identities may prove to be a mixed blessing. How important are such identities? Recall Rosenberg's observation: "The [Southern Baptist] Convention has consistently refused to change its name to anything less regional; the reasons for this have changed through time, but it has profound cultural meaning. Every time Southern Baptists have made this decision they have said something very important about who they want to be as well as who they are" (1989, 2). Following the merger, Hope Baptist chose to preserve and cultivate a region-based identity, at least in name, and this choice is important in that it may limit the church's appeal in this religiously plural central California community.

Hope Baptist's leadership is aware of that possibility. Virgil Johnson, the other copastor, speaks frankly about the liability of "southern" in a church's name outside the South. When missionary churches were started in California, they were called "First Southern Baptist Church of . . . ." Many of those names have subsequently changed, dropping the word "Southern." Some have even dropped "Baptist." When Johnson tried to assure me that there are prosperous Southern Baptist congregations in California (and indeed there are), he cited several, like Saddleback Valley Community Church in Orange County (which has more than 10,000 members), that dropped the "Southern" and "Baptist" altogether.

But identity is more than a name, and Hope Baptist's identity struggle is articulated not in terms of denominational affiliation or region per se but rather in terms of religious doctrine and morality, which are demarcating features of southern-style religion. Region, religion, and morality are in fact intertwined, and these California Southern Baptists are cultural conservatives. Hope Baptist Church is staunchly fundamentalist, a congregation of self-proclaiming "Bible believing" Christians that support "traditional family values." However, they appear to be winning no converts by asserting those values. Perhaps that should not be surprising. Whereas the traditional Christian morality they preach would be more or less an affirmation of southern culture, outside the South their fundamentalist message tends to repudiate the dominant culture, thus more often condemning than affirming the lifestyle of potential converts.

Pastor Taylor said in worship one morning, "This is a Baptist Church. If you didn't know that before you came in, you're going to know before you leave. . . . We believe in the Bible." Such proclamations may do more to gather in the faithful than to convert outsiders. Hope Baptist's pastors preach about the Bible, but they also condemn secular cultural trends. Sermons routinely contain messages that are anti-intellectual, antimaterialist, against popular culture—television in particular—and critical of the "new" morality. It is possible that such a message might convert those not reared Baptist or in some other evangelical tradition; people participate in church life for a variety of reasons. But Hope Baptist seems to be losing more than it gains by reasserting a conservative Christian moral agenda in Sunday worship.

In response to Taylor's criticism from the pulpit of the "liberal" shift in American political culture, one member complained: "There is too much politics in worship. I come to hear the Bible, not sermons on how the country is goin' to hell because the 'liberals' are in [power]." Most parishioners agree with the conservative sentiment, but the question of who outside the tradition will find that message appealing is critical to Hope Baptist's future.

Following the merger, the congregation hired a church growth consultant and developed a growth plan that included developing a vision for the newly formed church. This vision, printed on a large sign above the main entrance to the sanctuary, reads, "To glorify God by reaching and discipling young individuals and families." Along with focusing evangelistic energies, the congregation was encouraged to "modernize" worship and hire an outreach pastor. These steps, implemented a year prior to my research visits, may bear fruit eventually, but so far they appear to be meeting with limited success.

The new vision statement reflects congregants' ages. Like the congregations of most mainline Protestant churches, Hope's is graying. Like other churches, Hope is struggling to attract young people. However, revitalization will require more than printing the church's vision in the bulletin every week, and it is unclear how far the congregation is willing to go toward that end. For example, the consultant encouraged the church to become more contemporary in worship—to make services more participatory, to use a less formal liturgy, to present a more upbeat message—but such change is being resisted. When I asked Taylor about modernizing the worship experience, he replied simply, "We tried that one Sunday, and it didn't work." During the same conversation, he spoke of Robert Schuller's "contemporary style" disapprovingly. According to Taylor, Schuller strays too far from scripture, and his style of worship is too accepting of popular culture (that is, it is too materialistic and too embracing of the power-of-positive-thinking pop psychology). Another effort to update the worship experience involved hiring a male college student with shoulder-length hair to reinvigorate the music program, and his innovations were met with resistance. Congregants complained to the pastors that too few familiar hymns were being sung in worship.

Change does not come easily, and the strategy Hope Baptist settled on is what it calls a "blended" approach to worship and ministry, a style that its members say is not quite traditional but does not give in to contemporary trends (for example, guitar playing, holding hands, casual dress, overt emotionalism, and the like). Both Johnson and Taylor believe themselves to be middle-of-the-road in this respect, but their theological and moral vision and their style of conducting worship are sharply traditional compared to those of other Protestant churches in the community, and a majority of the congregation seems comfortable with that. These Baptists are advocates of a fundamentalist Christian faith and moral code in what they perceive to be a hostile secular environment. For all its talk of moderation and the blended approach to worship, this congregation has dug in its heels and assumed a defensive posture.

The new outreach pastor, Jack Holland, symbolizes the dilemma of old-time southern religion in California today. By hiring Holland, the church acknowledged the need to reach out to the community in a conciliatory way, but it is unable to do so. Holland is a bitter and outspokenly conservative man, which is an ominous sign for the church's new commitment to outreach. The world has "gone to hell," he claims, because people have moved away from the Bible—God's authority on moral and ethical questions. Young people are leaving the church and therefore have no morality, he further claims, which accounts for high crime rates, drug and alcohol abuse, homosexuality, and high divorce rates, among other "social problems."

Holland is a volunteer chaplain at a local hospital and notes with extreme frustration that there are no longer absolutes in medical ethics: "If three out of five health care workers agree that a medical procedure should be done, then it is, even if it is wrong." Holland describes his dismay at having the relatives of terminally ill people requesting to be present in the final moments so they can watch the soul depart, sure evidence of the demise of Christian morality and the growing influence of New Age religion. "Anything goes," he laments.

This traditionalism represents an oppositional stance toward the surrounding culture to a degree that Southern Baptists do not contend with in the South. While southern evangelicalism was never officially established, historically

> it enjoyed a privileged church-like status in Southern law and society. Blue laws established rules for Sunday conduct, and vice laws (including prohibition) gave evangelical morals legal force. Pastors routinely served as school chaplains, and Sunday School teachers populated the classrooms. No one ever seemed to complain about the prayer and Bible reading students did in school. There was enough religious homogeneity that people could act as if a consensus existed, disregarding the rules of civility that apply in more pluralistic setting and giving the region its appearance of pervasive religiosity. (Ammerman 1990, 55)

There is no remnant of an established evangelical culture outside the South, particularly in California. If southern churches in such areas are unable to adapt to the more pluralistic setting, they will struggle as Hope Baptist has done, and their appeal will be restricted to those who already share their sectarian values. It is precisely this tension with the temporal world that ultimately limits the appeal of southern religion outside the South, even if it prospered initially.

Moral and Theological Opposition to Secular Culture

When Hope Baptist asserts that it is a church of God-fearing, Bible-believing Christians, it is making moral as well as theological claims. That is the essential character of contemporary fundamentalism. The worldview it resists is moral relativism. It is responding not to a rise in atheism but to a perception that people no longer believe there are moral absolutes, while it appeals to the authority of God as revealed in the Bible to distinguish between right and wrong. Thus the real tension between these evangelicals and the wider community, sharpened in the case of Southern Baptists outside the South, is moral rather than theological.

No person in the new members' class, for instance, responded with much interest to the presentation of the doctrine of premillenial dispensationalism (complete with graphic depictions of the thousand-year reign of Christ and of Heaven and Hell), but everyone responded disapprovingly to the news that an SBC church in North Carolina was planning to perform a wedding ceremony for a homosexual couple. To the new members' class, which had an average of eight participants, only half of whom were new members (some, like the White's, were taking it as a refresher course), homosexuality was clearly unacceptable behavior and an important enough issue to prompt them to publicly voice their opposition.

The salience of morality over theology as the motivating force in this congregation is apparent in several ways. No member, for instance, needs to know the *Baptist Faith and Message* (the official statement of church doctrine) to be accepted at this church, and while members are expected to be born-again Christians, there is some latitude on what that means. No church leader checks born-again credentials, particularly in the case of someone who has been a lifelong Baptist. What is not acceptable, however, is behavior outside the church's vision of a moral life, particularly on issues relating to gender and sexuality. "I never thought I'd see the day," Taylor exhorted, "when Baptist churches would accept homosexuality. That's pathetic." His sermon on April 26, 1992, titled "Dealing with Serious Problems in the Church," was a message on sin, punishment, and "getting right with God." The reason we have such ungodliness, Taylor said, is that preachers refuse to preach "Thus saith the Lord." He insists that "we've gotten too liberal," that "things that were a sin twenty years ago are okay now. [We need to start] putting some shoe leather into the doctrine. You want to get a person right with God, but you don't do it by condoning sin. . . . [R]ebuking sinning believers is not optional; it is essential." By not only tolerating homosexuality but blessing the union of two gay men, the church in North Carolina, according to Taylor, is failing to root out sin within the Christian community. Taylor's message is one that most members of the congregation are comfortable with; it reaffirms rather than challenges their lifestyles.

During the 1980s, Taylor sat on a panel of local pastors that participated weekly in a community access television program designed to discuss moral and religious issues in the Central Coast. On the far left of the panel was the Unitarian minister, while Taylor was on the far right and often found himself defending Jerry Falwell and the Moral Majority, which he claims sometimes made him uncomfortable. Taylor was never a member of the Moral Majority and was ambivalent about the prominence of politics in the evangelical community during the 1980s, but he says he understands why some evangelicals felt the need to become more politically active. They did so in response to the ascendence of liberalism in American culture during the 1960s and 1970s. This is the same justification offered by the fundamentalists who have gained control in the Southern Baptist Convention over the last ten years. Conservatives are simply taking back what the liberals took from them in earlier years. Taylor views the actions of the Moral Majority in the 1980s, the new prominence of fundamentalists in SBC, and his own conservative stance on moral issues as defensive moves against the relentless forces of liberalism in the culture. He views himself as <u>reactive rather than proactive</u>, and he believes that nothing less than the moral character of American society is at stake. Taylor is not a Southern Baptist by cultural inheritance but rather a self-styled fundamentalist in sympathy with the conservative shift within the SBC.

Nor was Pastor Johnson reared a Southern Baptist, though he was educated at a Baptist college in Texas, and, like Taylor, seems to be most animated by moral issues. "If you want to stop people from having abortions," he says, "win them to God." The problem, he believes, is that "we've became [too] like the world." Hope Baptist and other southern churches outside the South confront the world—secular culture and moral relativism—more directly than their affiliates in the South, so the pressure on them to resist or accommodate social change is greater.

Hope Baptist is a southern church in important ways, but that has made this fundamentalist congregation marginal in the community; its diminishing status is probably related to its regional and conservative religious identity. This explanation seems more plausible in light of the recent emergence and growth of other, more contemporary evangelical churches in the community (see chapter 5).

On the other hand, it might be argued, this church is simply an anomaly, and making generalizations based on the experience of a single congregation is misleading if not irresponsible. Indeed, the SBC as a whole is still growing by about 2.5 percent annually (total membership in 1992 approached 16 million), but its rate of growth dropped in the last decade compared to its growth in the 1960s, '70s, and early '80s (*Southern Baptist Handbook* 1992). Slower growth among Southern Baptists is not surprising, it might be countered; they, like the members of Hope Baptist, are more fundamentalist than charismatic, and the real story of resurgent evangelicalism is the revival of charismatic Christianity. If so, we would expect that the Pentecostal congregations of the Assemblies of God, one of the largest non-Baptist "southern" church bodies, are prospering. I explore this issue in the next chapter.

CHAPTER FOUR

Praying for Revival
Portrait of a Struggling Pentecostal Church

In speaking of and praying for revival, it is important that we understand what we really desire and ask for. To most Christians the word conveys the meaning of a large increase in the number of conversions. When that happens, they say, "There has been quite a revival in that church (or town)." The true meaning of the word is far deeper. The word means making alive again those who have been alive but have fallen into what is called a cold, or dead, state.

Andrew Murry

New Life Christian Assembly (hereafter called New Life) is an Assemblies of God (AG) church located less than a mile from Hope Baptist Church. It is an impressive multibuilding complex, though more striking for its size than for its architectural merit. The main building, constructed in 1974, houses a large sanctuary, church offices, and adult education facilities. If the words *Worship Center* were absent above the front doors, the facility would be indistinguishable from other white stucco office buildings in the community. The sanctuary is modern compared to Hope Baptist's. Wooden pews are arranged in a 120-degree semicircle wrapping around the front altar and choir loft. Including the overhead balcony, the sanctuary comfortably seats perhaps five hundred people, but it is typically only one-third to one-half full on Sunday mornings.

The congregation is largely white, though several African American families attend on any given Sunday, as do several Hispanics and a number of people of Asian descent. In fact, this AG congregation is more ethnically diverse than most Protestant congregations in this community. There are slightly more women than men in regular attendance, and leadership roles in worship are sharply gender-segregated. The organist and pianist, for example, are women; the music director is a man. The twenty-person choir has a 4–1 ratio favoring women. The senior pastor and two associates are men. The ushers are always men, as are the deacons who assist with communion, and most of the Sunday school teachers are women. With respect to social class, the message from the pulpit is that all people are welcome, regardless of who they are, where they come from, or how they dress, but the ushers are always well dressed in suits that make them look like a group of successful businessmen; many are in fact professionals. In general, the women wear dresses or nice skirts and blouses. This is a solidly middle-class congregation that drives to worship services in late-model Toyotas, Volvos, Buicks, and Chryslers.

What is striking about the church setting just described is its familiarity to many American Protestants. New Life is white, middle-class, and suburban. It is still governed by traditional gender roles, has more members over forty years old than under, and has many empty pews during Sunday worship; in short, it looks and feels like a "mainline" church (Methodist, Lutheran, Presbyterian, and so on), but it is distinctly evangelical, and thus it is supposed to be growing.

New Life is the First Assemblies of God Church in this California community, and like its SBC neighbor, it too is an ailing congregation, one that grew dramatically during the 1960s and '70s but is losing members today. Its fundamentalist message and Pentecostal style of worship, two characteristic features of southern-style religion, contrast sharply with California's contemporary culture, which may be a clue to the church's diminishing membership. New Life is an evangelical congregation representing southern-style religion outside the South in three important ways. Organizationally, it is affiliated with the Assemblies of God, one of the largest non-Baptist southern religious organizations in the country. New Life began as an AG-supported storefront mission and still maintains that denominational tie. Second, its religious style is reminiscent of revivalistic Protestantism in the Old South. Like the Southern Baptists, the Assemblies of God are fundamentalist; they interpret the Bible literally and resist the encroachment of the secular world. But they are also Pentecostal, which is to say that they emphasize the gift of tongues, faith healing, and the imminent return of Christ. Theirs is a style of Protestant worship particularly at home in the South. Third, there are native-born southerners in this congregation for whom church affiliation is not an individual choice but rather a matter of cultural inheritance, persons reared in the Pentecostal tradition who had a multitude of religious options when they moved to California and yet sought out an Assemblies of God church. In its history, characters, and culture lie its identity as a specifically southern evangelical church and the reasons for its devitalization.

Vacant Pews in a "Living" Church

New Life started in 1939 as a downtown storefront mission, then called the Pentecostal Assembly. It was affiliated with the Missouri-based Assemblies of God. Faithful congregants built a small church on the east side of town in 1940, and for the next two decades the church grew at a slow but steady pace. Wendell Lewis was called to pastor the congregation in 1961 and agreed to come on the condition that the church relocate to a growing area in the community and launch a vigorous expansion campaign. The church moved to its present location on the west side of town in 1963. Lewis recalls that during the early days of his ministry, "people began experiencing Pentecost regularly in our services and the Lord began adding to our number continually." (Excerpt from a church history pamphlet written by Wendell Lewis, 1989.) The perception that people in the mainline denominations were becoming interested in the baptism of the Holy Spirit led to the establishment of a Monday evening charismatic meeting, which, Lewis further recalls, had "a distinct cross-denominational flavor." The congregation was still small, but according to Lewis, a spirit of revivalism characterized the early growth years.

The 1970s were boom years for New Life. In 1971 income increased 50 percent over the previous year, membership was up, construction of a children's center was completed, two Sunday morning services were being held, and additional land was purchased for the construction of a new sanctuary. Lewis's records show that 100 people received the baptism of the Holy Spirit in 1972, 33 were baptized in water that year, and there were 40 recorded first-time conversions. A new worship center was completed in 1974.

Growth continued throughout the 1970s and early '80s but leveled off in the mid-1980s as the congregation and its pastor matured. Division within the church following Lewis's retirement after nearly thirty years of service resulted in a drop in membership and income between 1989 and 1991. Of the 533 people added to the church roll between 1970 and 1980, fewer than 75—about 15 percent—still attend. A majority of current members joined the church since 1985. Church income increased dramatically during the 1970s and most of the 1980s and peaked at over a half-million dollars in 1987. Income has fallen off in recent years, dropping from $495,000 in 1989 to $384,000 in 1990.

New Life's dramatic membership loss in the late 1980s was related to congregational life-cycle dynamics—the maturation of the congregation, the routinization of worship (the "comfortable pew" phenomenon; see Berton 1965), and internal power struggles, particularly around the issue of what kind of leader should replace the outgoing pastor. It is important to note, however, that these issues are substantially cultural as well as organizational.

When the congregation failed to hire Robert Anthony as Lewis's replacement after he had served the church for a trial year, the congregation divided, and several dozen members left in loyalty to Anthony, a man described as an old-style, Bible-storytelling pastor whose primary concern was tending the flock rather than carrying the gospel of Jesus Christ to the world. Peter Stone was eventually hired as the senior pastor, primarily for his evangelistic skills. The congregation charged him with the task of regenerating in the church and in the community at large the spirit of revivalism, a spirit characteristic of its southern evangelical heritage and consistent with Stone's background as a second-generation Pentecostal preacher. Under Stone's leadership, New Life is committed to stemming the tide of membership loss by returning to its Pentecostal roots.

A New Preacher, An Uncertain Future

The long-lived stereotypical image of Pentecostals is that they are less well educated then most people, tend to come from rural backgrounds, particularly in the South, and are unequivocally antimodern. In short, they are seen as religious fanatics left over from a bygone era. Sociological research in the middle decades of the twentieth century that linked Protestant sectarianism with low social standing tended to reinforce this portrait. Indeed, there is a defensive self-awareness of the stereotype among New Life church members themselves, particularly the new pastor, which they are eager to dispel. The picture emerging from my research at New Life contradicts such stereotypes—the congregation is middle-class, and there is a complex blending of modern culture with religious tradition—but old-time religion is nevertheless theologically and morally intact in this AG congregation. The new pastor exemplifies the church's mixing of two cultures (traditional and modern, southern and nonsouthern), but he also clearly illustrates New Life's reaffirmation of its revivalistic roots.

Stone's spacious church office is better organized and has more books than most academics' offices. Along with the writings of D. L. Moody, histories of religious revival in America, and church growth studies are books like John Naisbitt's *Megatrends* and Robert Bellah et al., *Habits of the Heart*. Stone has an undergraduate degree from a Missouri Bible college, where he studied history. He later attended Whittier Seminary and is currently a doctoral candidate at Fuller Theological Seminary in Pasadena, California, one of the most prestigious and most modern evangelical seminaries in the country.

Stone is educated and articulate; he drives a Lincoln Continental, belongs to a health club, and keeps himself physically fit. "I play racketball, lift weights, and like women—especially my wife," he reported during one conversation, as if to say, "We Pentecostals are as with it as the next guy." Indeed, Stone is. Before coming to this community, he served a San Diego Assemblies of God church for twelve years. In his words, it was, when he arrived, a "beachy" community of thirty people, "young, laid-back, and braless." Under his leadership the church grew to several hundred, about half of them single.

With more than a dozen years in Southern California, Stone knows this version of modern life, is in many ways shaped by it, and yet resists it. Underneath several layers of modern manners, he has a spirit of intense Christian traditionalism. This traditionalism is reflected in his view of life in California, which he describes as chaotic and utterly secular: "When I talk to people on the streets, they're pagan. They don't even know who Jesus Christ is. LA reminds me of the talk about 'principalities' discussed in the Book of Daniel"—a region inhabited by demonic forces. "This place is in need of revival," he went on to say, "and it is going to take a miracle to make it happen. . . . And nothing is going to happen unless the spirit of God does something." Stone's traditionalism is also expressed in a consistently sharp critique of materialism in American society. He is not among those contemporary evangelicals who have embraced the materialistic rewards of American capitalism—there are no prayers for extended vacations in the Caribbean—and yet he drives a luxury automobile and vacations in Palm Springs. In his sermons, he often refers to the "early church" as a model of commitment and simplicity. He is a modern man with traditional sensibilities.

Stone's Christian traditionalism is rooted in a pious family background. His father was an evangelist who came from a family of farmers ("horse traders and horse thieves," Stone jokingly says), was "saved" at the age of sixteen, and studied in the itinerant tradition of D. L. Moody at a Bible college in Zion, Illinois. Because his father founded more than a dozen churches in Wisconsin and Michigan during his lifetime, the younger Stone spent his whole childhood in and around Pentecostal churches and was nurtured in a Christian home. Ex-president Jimmy Carter once described his religious background in the following terms: "It was part of my life like breathing, like being a Georgian or being a human being. To be part of a church, like to be a Christian, was just assumed as a natural part of life." The same could be said for Peter Stone; his Pentecostalism is as much a part of his inheritance as is the color of his skin.

However, while Stone is loyal to this heritage—at least its core—his faith is not quite the old-time religion of his father's era. Stone and his congregants are far more educated than the members of his father's churches. They are primarily urban rather than rural people, and they lack the crass emotionalism characteristic of the early waves of charismatic revival that his father was a part of in the 1930s, '40s, and '50s. Stone's beliefs are more sophisticated, and his style is more subdued, yet he remains loyal to the faith of his ancestors in his emphasis on a personal commitment to Christ made manifest in the visible power of the Holy Spirit.

The legacy of old-time religion is apparent in Stone's preaching in his emphasis on "right living" for faithful Christians. In one sermon, entitled "Making Up: Reconciliation," he called upon the congregation to heal the wounds that had been opened in the recent staff controversy. In a setting of some conflict and bitterness, it was clearly a message on forgiveness, yet the sermon moved back and forth between a call for reconciliation among congregants and a call for sinners to repent, between mending community and individual accountability before God. "The family of God is not only a healing community but is also a holy community," Stone noted in his sermon summary, printed in the bulletin. "It dispenses compassion and maintains accountability with equal diligence." Reconciliation between people occurs only by the grace of God and only after individuals get right with God. The church has a responsibility, it was suggested, to purge the congregation of sinners who are unwilling to repent. They can be welcomed back into the fold only after acknowledging their sinfulness before God. The message is that corporate problems are merely the aggregate of individual sins.

Following the series on forgiveness, Stone preached for two months on the importance of prayer in Christian life. His message on prayer was not about contemplation or reflection so much as a method for doing spiritual battle against Satan—a tool for fighting evil.

The language of old-time religion is everywhere apparent in these sermons on prayer. Stone sees prayer as the key to revitalizing his struggling new congregation and ultimately the only way to bring about change in a secular and increasingly immoral society. Prayer is a way that believers call on the power of God to intercede in the lives of troubled individuals or the behavior of entire communities. Waging spiritual battle is essential in a world influenced by demonic forces, powers that can be combatted only with the power of the Holy Spirit. Stone's sermon "Christ's Invitation to Intercessors" (December 1, 1991) stressed the importance of prayer in the following terms:

> If the church is going to go forward, it's going to go forward on its knees. . . . The history of the Church is the history of prayer. If we're going to go forward, we're going to go forward in prayer because there is a link between prayer and the power of the Holy Spirit. . . . Without power [of the Holy Spirit] it is impossible for us to attack the strongholds of the enemy in this world: disease, despair, disillusionment, dismay, and destruction . . . and the dishonesty, and deceit, and divorce, and the dismay of people who have tried everything only to be disappointed and on the verge of death.

How can the Church be powerful in a community? the pastor asked rhetorically. How can it fight the forces of the enemy? Through prayer and intercession, he answered; that is the only way to bring about social change.

I would like you to think about [your community. It] is an outpost, and it is controlled by not just political figures, but there are spiritual forces at work. And as we begin to look at our church, it is not just a matter of going out and convincing people that we have the truth, but we are going to go out and contend with spiritual forces. And we are going to go out and establish bases of operations. And I am using military language because that's in fact what we are about. We are a part of a military force. We are guerrillas invading the enemy territory.

Prayer is the weapon of spiritual warfare. The sermon worksheet in the bulletin that day began by quoting the Christian evangelist Dr. Hallisby: "In prayer the churches receive power to rule the world. The Church is always a little flock. But if it would stand together on its knees, it would dominate world politics—from the prayer room." Stone's "new" message to his congregation— aimed at revitalizing the community—is an old one: prepare to do battle with Satan, and prepare to see religious revival in the region. There is an imperative here to change the world, but by prayer rather than politics:

> Become a soldier. Get the eyes of a soldier. Look around your community. Begin to pray. Seek God. Where are the strongholds that are in our community? And God will begin to show you certain places in this community that he . . . wants you to minister to.
>
> What are we talking about when we talk about spiritual warfare? We are identifying places where Satan has his hold. I'm talking about, it could be abused children in our community. . . . Or there may be other things. You may be moved, some of you already are, moved toward the great sin of murder and abortion in our area. And you begin to pray, and others will gather around you, and you will begin to identify and intercede against that. . . . And we push back the gates of hell as each of us begins to go out and come against the enemy.

This language is not much different from the evangelical battle cries on the American frontier a century and a half ago. The itinerant Baptist preachers in the South and West at the turn of the nineteenth century were chasing the devil out of the wilderness. Today Pentecostals and other conservative Protestants like those at New Life still sound the battle cry. The language is the same, only now the wilderness is modern urban America.

There is a second meaning to Stone's message on the importance of prayer; it has to do with reinvigorating the faithful and deepening their Christian commitment. He wants to arouse a spirit of Christian revivalism in the sense described in the opening passage from Andrew Murry's book *Revival* (1990), quoted as this chapter's epigraph. American Pentecostalism is an outgrowth of episodes of charismatic revival at the turn of the century. Stone's call for a spirit of revival among congregants echoes this past.

Stone's focus on revival has less to do with numbers of people in the pews than it does with the depth of members' commitments. If those who are active take their faith—their evangelistic call— seriously, then the congregation will grow as a matter of course. Stone's long-range vision is to "call people to be disciples and to have them go out and make new disciples." Simple conversion to the faith is not the objective, however; a high level of commitment to a congregation is. "We don't want to build on 'groups,' promotional deals, or PR. The modern way is to get on TV and save the same person twenty times over. That's how they get such high 'conversion' rates," Stone laments. He is somewhat cynical about televangelism and the megachurch phenomenon because, in his view, to be a disciple one must belong to a community of believers: "A person isn't a disciple until he or she is active in a congregation." He does see value in celebrity benefits for the community for social service, but not for the purpose of church growth. "We don't want people to join because a movie star attends. The commitment is too fragile." He prefers people with high commitment and low visibility to those with low commitment and high visibility. "This," he says, "is how Jesus started his ministry."

While Stone is deeply committed to church growth, it will not be at the cost of lowering his standards of Christian commitment. He attended a church growth seminar in Sacramento this fall with George Barna, author of *User Friendly Churches,* and Bill Hybels, founder of Willow Creek Community Church—a megachurch catering to young suburban professionals that was shaped by "customer" polls and marketing strategies. Stone is quite critical of the service-station model of churches and church growth. His model is the "early church" (first-century Christians), which was made up of a small but fiercely committed band of followers. Stone would rather pastor a few highly committed disciples of Christ then a mass of what he refers to as "Sunday morning Christians." He reasons that a small group of strong believers can, in the long run, more successfully disciple others in the community than throngs of marginally committed worshipers. And achieving this, he believes, requires prayer and following scripture.

Another component of Stone's traditionalism is his fundamentalist interpretation of scripture. In his view, the Bible is literally God's word and the final authority on matters of faith and obedience to God. On this point Stone does not waver, and he intends to hold people accountable for their behavior. Christians must follow the scripture, and the church is there to help them do so. Being a Christian is not an easy road, Stone says. If, for example, a husband is thinking of divorcing his wife, the church is going to step in and counsel against it. That is what we are told in scripture, Stone says. After introducing the *Statement of Fundamental Truths* (the statement of Assemblies of God doctrine) to the new members' class, Stone said, with a sardonic smile, that when outsiders "talk about fundamentalists, they are talking about us."

Through prayer, discipleship, and allegiance to the word of God, Stone is trying to instill a spirit of Christian revivalism among New Life faithful. *His* church is struggling in central California, and *the* Church is struggling in the world. Faithful Christians, according to Stone, need to get back to the basics. This call, however, is problematic. Pentecostals at New Life, like their new pastor, are theologically and morally conservative, and yet they live inescapably modern lives, particularly in this California setting. Nonetheless, the worship experience at New Life is traditional Pentecostal.

Southern Pentecostals Outside the South

Following the organ prelude that begins a typical worship service at New Life, the likeness between this church and a liberal Protestant church quickly fades. The music director leads the congregation in twenty to thirty minutes of spirited singing of contemporary "praise songs" mixed with traditional hymns (for example, "All Hail the Power of Jesus' Name" and "Amazing Grace") selected from the same hymnal that is used by the Southern Baptist church. The praise music, much of it written in the last ten years, is focused on glorifying Jesus Christ ("He Is Lord," "Lord of My Heart," "He is Exalted On High") and is generally upbeat, inspirational, and reiterative, often drawing emotional and sometimes physical responses from worshippers. It is not uncommon for people to sing with their hands raised in the air, palms turned upward, eyes closed, and bodies swaying to the music.

A short opening prayer by Stone generally follows, and it is marked by passion and sincerity. Stone's voice cracks and grows thin when he prays for the well-being of people in the congregation who are sick or whose lives are otherwise troubled. He is often overcome with emotion—typically a kind of despairing sadness stemming from a feeling of unworthiness—during worship, especially during prayers.

The opening prayer is followed by congregational announcements. At this time one Sunday during the period I observed the church, the chairperson of the prayer committee announced that he needed people to sign up to pray between midnight and 6:00 AM as part of a week-long congregational focus on prayer for the surrounding community. They were instructed to pray that the forces of light defeat the forces of darkness in the world. The plan was to have someone from the church praying at every hour of the day and through the night. Pastor Stone supported the request by saying, "Let's have an evangelistic call. Who wants to set their alarm and get up in the middle of the night to pray?" Working like an auctioneer, he solicited commitments for every half-hour slot for the six-hour period. There was reluctance at first, but once the call picked up momentum, volunteers' hands shot up. Stone finished by saying, "We're serious. We believe in prayer. And you are going to see the fruits of this."

Announcements are followed by special music. One Sunday, for example, a young black woman from the congregation sang "Jesus, the Friend of a Wounded Heart," a song about the comfort to be found in committing oneself to Jesus Christ. On other Sundays, guests—born-again evangelists with traveling music ministries—may be invited to entertain and inspire the congregation. The message of most of this music is the promise of individual salvation, of mending a broken life.

Prior to the pastor's sermon, there is an interlude of five to ten minutes for prayer and openness to the movement of the Holy Spirit, prefaced by the pastor's saying, "Lord, your power is released." People close their eyes and begin praying aloud, many with uplifted hands. There is commotion as earnest voices call out "Almighty God," "Hallelujah," "Yes, Jesus," "We Glorify Your Name," "Praise God." This is a time when the "moaners and groaners" of the congregation surface, as one parishioner described them. During this prayer time, a voice might ring out, saying, "I am the Lord Your God . . ." and a prophecy ensue admonishing congregants to halt their evil ways and get right with God. The tone and style are usually scriptural, meant to sound like an Old Testament prophet or God Himself calling His people to obedience. (I use the male pronoun here because it is conventional in this church.) On rare occasions someone in the congregation might speak in tongues and be interpreted by another congregant.

While some features of New Life, particularly its empty pews, remind one of a faltering mainline church, this congregation is decidedly evangelical. Scripture is treated here as the literal word of God and the final authority in all matters of consequence; a born-again experience (a commitment or recommitment to Jesus) is expected of all true believers, which will be followed by baptism in the Holy Spirit as evidenced by the recipient's speaking in unknown tongues; and there is an obligation to share this faith with others so that they too may find salvation, though some parishioners have more zeal than others for this mandate. How deep is the evangelical commitment in this church?

Stone is a charismatic preacher, lively and articulate. He invokes the language of old-time religion in his sermons to encourage church members to be more than "Sunday morning Christians." The Christian life should be a total life, Stone says. His message is followed by an offering and another hymn, and the service closes with an invitation. During the altar call, the congregation sings "Just as I Am" or "At the Cross," classic hymns used by the Southern Baptists at the same point in their worship service.

New Life is a second illustration of the southernization process described in aggregate terms in chapter 2. Like Hope Baptist, New Life is a southern church outside the South that grew during the 1970s when evangelicalism gained new prominence in the culture at large, but now it too is a congregation in decline. I suggest that the weakening of both these evangelical churches must be understood in light of their region-based identity. They are still southern churches organizationally and culturally, a status that served them well initially in that it enabled them to gather in displaced southerners familiar with their religious beliefs and practices, but over time their southernness appears to have become a liability in California's open religious marketplace.

Inheriting Evangelicalism

To argue that New Life is a southern church is to suggest that Southerners belong to its congregation, and indeed they do, though, as in Hope Baptist Church, their numbers are small today. Most of these members, like their pastor, are people who have inherited evangelicalism; their affiliation expresses ascriptive religious preferences. Of the several dozen worshippers I spoke with on Sunday mornings over a three-month period, a majority were reared conservative Protestant, though not necessarily in the South, and the rest were "saved" as adults. Yet the presence of Southerners in a southern church outside the South explains only the *spread* of evangelicalism, not its growth in absolute terms. Though there are other reasons people join an evangelical church, it is interesting to look first at people who do so because they are southern evangelicals or were reared in other conservative Protestant churches.

While one can routinely hear the name of Jesus being praised with a southern accent and occasionally spot someone wearing jeans, boots, and a bolo tie, there are fewer obvious signs of southern culture at New Life than can be found in the Hope Baptist congregation. I met people from Oklahoma, Missouri (the AG headquarters), Arkansas, Mississippi, and states adjacent to southern ones (Illinois and Kansas). Most people at New Life, in other words, are not southerners. Yet there is more than an echo of the old-time religion here. Certainly many who have found a home here were themselves nurtured in a conservative Protestant tradition, often in the South.

Among the most distinctive features of New Life's Sunday worship—the thing that most obviously suggests old-time religion—is the deep and resounding voice of southerner Luke Berry, whose expressions of praise accent the period of prayer before the sermon: "Amen!" "We praise your name, Jesus!" "We thank you, almighty God!" "Hallelujah!" "Glory be to God!" His southern drawl is unmistakable in the chorus of spontaneous praise on Sunday morning. Berry was born and raised in the predominately Baptist culture of Alabama but was not saved until he met the woman who became his wife, a born-again Church of God member. For a quarter-century, Luke and Sarah Berry pastored churches in the Midwest and states bordering the South. They moved to California in the early 1980s to serve a church in Bakersfield, California, then moved to Central Coast two years ago. Luke Berry's present faith, like that of most New Life parishioners, is an extension of his religious past, a result of his being reared in the Christian culture of the South.

Richard King and Jack Hope, two longtime New Life members, exemplify especially well the type of New Life member who has inherited evangelicalism. They both adhere to the evangelical tradition, though perhaps the only thing they have in common is their longstanding faith. King is a prominent black member of the wider community and has attended New Life since he and his family moved there in 1975. He is a public education administrator and a past president of the local NAACP chapter; he is currently serving a two-year term as president of his national professional association. His undergraduate and graduate degrees are from major research universities.

The son of a devout Pentecostal preacher in Arkansas, King has a rich evangelical heritage. His grandfathers were both Methodist churchmen, one a preacher and the other a deacon. Of his twelve siblings, three brothers are Pentecostal preachers—two of them in California. The church he grew up in was part of the Church of God in Christ—a segregated outgrowth of the Pentecostal movement in the early twentieth century. According to King, in the South the Assemblies of God Fellowship (AGF) is a "white" church; the Church of God in Christ (CGC) is its "black" counterpart. Following his graduate work, King took a job in Missouri and settled in a town with no CGC congregation. Wanting to stay close to his Pentecostal roots, he joined an Assemblies of God congregation, along with his family. When they moved to central California in 1975, they joined New Life because it was the largest AG church in town and had a thriving youth program. King's church affiliations over the years are a story of allegiance to his Pentecostal heritage. Though his faith is undoubtedly different from that of his father, who had only a tenth-grade education, King's devout Christian rearing set a faith trajectory from which he has not wavered.

Though he fits the pattern of displaced southerners affiliating with southern churches outside the South, King is not a conservative like most white New Life members and southern evangelicals generally. He is not a friend of the Christian Right, and he says that there are things about the Assemblies of God generally and this church specifically that are too conservative for his taste; they take positions on social issues that he disagrees with. But overall, he is still comfortable with Pentecostalism and enjoys worshiping at New Life. Like the faith of Stone and Jimmy Carter, King's faith is part of his inheritance.

Jack Hope is King's ideological opposite, but he also inherited his religious faith through family and cultural history. Hope, who is about seventy years old, is white, was raised in Oregon (rather than in the South) by an atheist father, has no college education (his children, however, are white-collar professionals), has done blue-collar work most of his life (including stints as a logger and a farmer), and has the missionary zeal of a devout evangelical Christian.

After a trip to Springfield, Missouri, in October 1991, Hope gave a testimonial on his experience worshiping with Christians in other Assemblies of God churches (Springfield is the national headquarters of the AGF). Hope's message was striking because he spoke joyfully and with vigor as he bounced around the pulpit proclaiming the Christian faith to be strong across the land. He is an exemplar of "living faith"; his style that of an old-time evangelist.

Hope sees himself as an inheritor of evangelicalism despite his father's atheism. He had no religious training as a child but was saved at the age of twenty-four by an itinerant Pentecostal evangelist during a weekend revival meeting in a rural southern Oregon town. Though his father was not a believer, his grandfather William Henry Hope was a circuit-riding minister of the Gospel. William Henry Hope was born in Sycamore, Illinois, in 1848 and moved to Oregon to preach the Gospel. Hope has reconstructed bits of his grandfather's life history, which he uses in his ministry to others. Following is an excerpt from the story he tells:

> William's zeal for Jesus was apparent at an early age, we are told, and continued throughout this difficult ministry for God. At an early age, William experienced the reality of Romans 10:9–10 and always emptied his coin purse for the cause of Christ. As a teenager, William was a strong witness of Matthew 10:32 and made pledges of money for the work of God, often hard to keep. Around 1868, William Henry became a minister of the saddlebag era, riding the Coos County [Oregon] circuit. . . . His experiences with mud, snow, and winter floods and storms give a glimpse into the almost incredible hardships endured in that early day. However, William's Pentecostal witness and love for the heavenly language and supernatural offering of money and self made him a very unusual man of God.

Hope views his own Christian faith as continuous with the faith of his forbearers, and that history is important to him. He says that his father rebelled against his own father's Christian beliefs, and perhaps Jack Hope's piety and missionary zeal are a rejection of his father's atheism. Whether or not this is true, Hope sees himself as carrying on a tradition, and his model for ministry is his itinerant evangelical grandfather.

The evangelical faith was reinforced in Hope's marriage to a Christian woman who is a native Oklahoman. She too experienced a Pentecostal baptism as a young adult. Jack and Margaret Hope have three children, all of whom are grown, have families of their own, and are actively involved in Pentecostal churches. The faith has been passed on to the next generation. Hope and his immediate family do not associate with his Oregon kin—his father's side of the family—because, he says, "they aren't Christians"; but Jack and Margaret were among Christian friends during their two-week Missouri vacation. They stayed at a Christian retreat center called Jubilee and from there made excursions into Arkansas and Oklahoma to visit friends and family, all "good Christian folks," Hope reports.

All this is to suggest that the Hopes' faith is very much derivative of old-time religion. Jack Hope is a Bible believer whose faith is displayed in the gifts of the spirit, and his highest calling on this earth is the salvation of wayward souls. He is a charismatic fundamentalist, and his missionary zeal gives character and direction to his daily life. Hope is a self-taught preacher and believes that seminaries—"cemeteries," he jokingly calls them—are spiritually dead places. His faith is nurtured not in theological reflection but through prayer to a living God who is miraculous and visible in the world and through constant reference to the Bible, the inerrant word of God.

Comforting the Brokenhearted

Some New Life members were not raised Pentecostal; they are "converts" coming from diverse backgrounds—different regions of the country, different levels of education, and different social classes—but there is a common thread in their conversion stories. Conversion to an evangelical faith tends to occur at times of personal crisis when people are struggling to piece their lives together without a supporting and affirming community. Evangelical communities provide an ideology and social environment in which some people find solace and the strength to rebuild their lives. Evangelicals are comforters of the brokenhearted. The following three portraits of New Life converts illustrate this type of evangelical character.

Mike Cooper is a troubled man, not at ease with the world around him. He is perhaps forty years old, a high school dropout, twice divorced, and currently engaged to be married again. Cooper drives a worn 1974 Toyota Corolla with an "I ❤ Jesus" sign dangling from the rearview mirror. The bumper sports a

"God Bless the Troops" sticker, a reference to the Persian Gulf War.

I interviewed Cooper in a coffee shop. He arrived a bit anxious, carrying a copy of the book *Satan's Underground: The Extraordinary Story of One Woman's Escape*. He describes his life as a road full of potholes and wrong turns, including the periodic contemplation of suicide. He is currently unemployed but was most recently a painter on the maintenance crew at a local Christian college, a job he held for five years but did not enjoy. He appears to be a physically healthy man, but he reports being on disability and under a doctor's care for stress-related illness. Cooper says he needs to make a living, yet he has no job prospects or much direction. "God has a plan for my life," he says reassuringly, but he is unclear about what the plan is.

Mike Cooper describes his childhood in Indiana as unpleasant; he says he never felt comfortable with his family or his peers. He recalls feeling unwanted and unloved. His father had no interest in religion and, Cooper claims, told his sons he would sooner see them mixed up with drugs than hanging out with Jesus freaks. At sixteen Cooper was caught trying to steal a car. That landed him a probation term and, in lieu of jail, a two-year stint in the Marine Corps, from which he received a dishonorable discharge. He has hitchhiked around the country and lived on the streets, and he describes being saved at a meeting of the Lighter Side of Darkness, an organization of the Jesus People movement of that era, in 1973 in Illinois. His conversion experience included praying in tongues. However, he recalls seven years of backsliding on his commitment to Christ following it, at which time he went back to using drugs and hanging out with "the wrong people."

The world is an evil place to Mike Cooper. "Don't you feel a heaviness, a darkness over the area, something oppressive?" he asks during an interview. "Satan is at work right here in [this community]." He described Satan's presence as pervasive and palpable, almost something one could reach out and touch. He talked about three hundred different cults in the area and described Dianetics (the Church of Scientology) as a front for devil worshippers. Satanists pervade the area, he believes, especially in the wealthy section of town because residents of that neighborhood tend to be doctors and lawyers—powerful people whose resources allow them to cover up their satanic work. For Cooper the devil is everywhere, and the way to combat his evil is through prayer and calling on the power of God. Cooper invokes the same language of spiritual warfare that one hears from the pulpit—"waging battle with the enemy." Satan is attacked by praying for the salvation of lost souls and sharing the message of the Gospel with people we know who are being tempted daily. Listening to Cooper describe the battle he is helping wage conjures up an image of armor-clad spirits of light and darkness mounted on horses and jousting in the sky above. It seems real to him. Cooper is not hopeful about the battle with Satan here on earth. His consolation is that believing Christians will have their way in the afterlife, leaving the unsaved to burn in hell.

While Cooper had some Catholic training in his childhood, he has no strong sense of being reared in a religious tradition of any stripe. He is a convert, someone coming into the fold from outside the conservative Protestant tradition. He has attended New Life off and on for ten years but clearly has no denominational allegiance. He has attended more than half a dozen Pentecostal and fundamentalist churches in the area, including the Foursquare Gospel Church and both Vineyard congregations. He is a born-again Christian; that is all that is important to him.

Tom Lang is in many ways Mike Cooper's opposite. He is better educated, comes from a solid (though not strongly Christian) family background, is happily married, is successful in his work, and is a much less troubled man than Cooper, though his assessment of the world and his vision of the future are similarly laced with apocalyptic themes. He is tall, gentle, open, and friendly, secure in his own faith and not pushy in his witness to others. He is a man of conviction and humility.

Lang grew up in Washington State. His parents were not religious, but he and his siblings were often dropped at his grandparents' on Sunday mornings and taken to Sunday school at the Church of Christ. There he heard Bible stories as a youngster and was baptized at age twelve, but he lost all interest in the church as a young teen. His parents, he recalls, didn't encourage him one way or the other. He was a basketball star in high school and college, which brought popularity and an active party life that included experimentation with sex, drugs, and alcohol. For a time he was a heavy alcohol user, which, he says, brought him unhappiness as well as euphoria. He recalls feeling that something was missing, that he wasn't satisfied with his life, that there had to be more to it than athletic success, drug highs, or what he describes as shallow relationships with women.

When Lang was nineteen years old and working at an oil refinery, he was introduced to Jesus Christ "in a personal way" by a Christian man whom he recalls with admiration. When Lang came to work drunk, the man, whom he called Jess, would talk with him in a sincere and caring way without condemning him. Gradually, Jess shared with Lang his own faith in the Gospel. After some months, Jess invited Lang to his home for dinner, where, as Lang recalls, they "said a simple prayer that changed my life." Lang was most impressed by Jess because he *lived* his faith; Christianity was not just a creed to him. Lang said he did not feel bombarded with scripture or moral judgment. The effect of this experience is evident in his own Christian ministry. Witnessing his faith does not involve Bible-thumping or beating the unsaved over the head with the good news, as he puts it.

Following his conversion, Lang became involved with Campus Crusade for Christ at the college he attended and eventually joined an Assemblies of God congregation in the area. He wanted to be part of a "spiritually alive" church, and the local AG congregation offered such a worship environment. Lang is not denominationally bound and says that he found the Assemblies of God Fellowship an attractive church body because the worship styles he found there were diverse within the parameters of evangelical Christianity. Eventually he became very involved with campus ministry and moved into a leadership role. He meet his wife, Tammy (who was reared a Baptist in Texas), in the Campus Crusade group. They married five years later, and both left secure, well-paid jobs to move to California and pursue their call to Christian ministry. Tom is now the campus minister for University Christian Fellowship, an Assemblies of God affiliate group.

Kathleen Starr, a women in her mid fifties, is a longtime New Life member. She was raised in West Virginia and migrated with her husband to this California community thirty-three years ago. They brought no specific religious tradition with them, only cultural Christianity. Starr is always well dressed, drives a luxury automobile, and comes to worship by herself. She says she was saved thirteen years ago, a month after one of her sons became a born-again Christian. She was an alcoholic before her conversion, and she says that her life has changed dramatically as a result of her acceptance of Jesus Christ. She reports with regret that her husband is not saved, and only one of her five children is a Christian.

The backgrounds of Cooper, Lang, and Starr are worlds apart, yet they share the experience of having converted to Christianity—born-again style— at crisis points in their lives. All three attribute their current stability and happiness to that change. Their evangelical faith is helping them rebuild and redirect their lives. To borrow a phrase from pastor Stone, they have "become victors instead of victims. What has happened in the past is gone and forgotten. [They] have become new men [and women] in Jesus Christ."

One critical feature of their new stability is the discipline that accompanies evangelical religion. While conservative theology and personal piety may not be the reasons people are born again and join a church like New Life— Cooper, Lang, and Starr converted simply because they were hurting or unhappy—they nonetheless all express more or less traditional Christian values that stand in stark contrast to the secular culture surrounding New Life. These evangelicals speak of the devil, the word of God, and the importance of being born again, but one wonders whether their evangelical zeal is as much moral as it is religious. For all their "God talk," the issues that most exercise this Christian community are moral issues, particularly around sexuality and changing gender roles.

Christians in a Sinful World

Whatever else religion is, it is always social and therefore cultural; it expresses morality as well as theological meaning. Following is an excerpt from field notes that illustrates the primacy of sexual morality over spirituality that characterizes New Life's Christian faith and message.

There was a special prayer for healing this morning. Pastor Stone invited the congregation to join in prayer for the health of a five-year-old girl who is inexplicably ill and in a constant state of exhaustion. The mother rose from her seat and walked toward the front of the sanctuary carrying her limp, slumbering daughter. With a faint smile on her face, she had a look of concern, expectancy, and gratitude. The child was wearing a short dress that, because of the awkward way she was cradled by her mother, exposed her thighs, backside, and underpants. The pastor came out from behind the pulpit to meet the mother and daughter as they approached. The mother's attention was focused on the pastor; she seemed unaware of and unconcerned about her daughter's appearance. When she and the pastor met in front of the pulpit and turned to face the congregation, the pastor fumbled with the dress and partially succeed in covering the girl's exposed body. The pastor's action was composed and graceful, but he was clearly made uneasy by the girl's appearance. There was an awkward moment. Then the mother helped rearrange the dress, and the pastor placed his hand on the child's head and began to pray for healing. There was no appearance of miraculous change in the girl, and the mother and daughter returned to their pew.

This episode may seem trivial, and indeed it may be. But it may also be emblematic of the moral issues that animate the New Life congregation—among them the belief that nudity is always vulgar. In fact, this episode is reminiscent of Francis Fitzgerald's description of the salience of morality compared to theology that she observed in Jerry Falwell's fundamentalist community in Virginia:

The pastors and pastoral students at the Thomas Road Baptist Church conceive of their activities in theological terms and could, if called upon, justify any one of them by a Biblical quotation. All the same, . . . to see a pastor remind a little girl to put underpants on her baby brother is to see that they are involved in a world of appearances, social forms, and personal behavior at some remove from Biblical history and at some remove from the direct mystical experience of Christ. For them, getting "saved" is clearly only the first step. It is true that most clergymen of all faiths are involved with the conduct of daily life, but the Thomas Road pastors—and fundamentalist pastors generally—have a much more specific and detailed set of prescriptions for the conduct of everyday life than do most Protestant churchmen. They have—like many Southern Baptists—absolute prohibitions against drink, tobacco, drugs, cursing, dancing, rock and roll, and extramarital sex, but they also have specific prescriptions for dress, child rearing, and the conduct of a marriage. (1986, 136–40)

Pastor Stone is also concerned with appearances and has prescriptions for right conduct. What are the moral issues in this congregation? And most important, what power does the church have over its parishioners to sanction immoral behavior? The answer to this last question is important for understanding the role this Pentecostal church plays in the wider community, a role I see as ultimately limited by inflexible positions on moral issues in a context of relative tolerance for alternative lifestyles.

The Assemblies of God Fellowship as a whole tends to be morally conservative. The February 2, 1992, issue of the national church's weekly magazine, *Pentecostal Evangel,* which is available in the New Life narthex on Sunday mornings, featured several articles about sexual morality that indicate the church's official position on this matter. It contains an autobiographical account of the evils of homosexuality in which the author writes, "I want other homosexuals to know there is a way out of the darkness into the light—and that way is through Jesus Christ." The lead article, "Talking about AIDS at Home," suggests that "we should speak of sex in the light of God's goodness and regard lust as Satan's warping of God's provision." Adultery, fornication, homosexuality, and incest are regarded as "sins of the flesh." A third article, written by a medical doctor and titled "The Myth of *Safe* Sex," suggests there is nothing safe about sex when it is practiced in the way recommended by safe-sex advocates. The author writes,

The personal tragedy that has struck Magic Johnson notwithstanding, the real tragedy is that the ensuing discussion occurred in a moral vacuum. It was stripped of values. The wrongness of extramarital sexuality was ignored, the rightness of abstinence ridiculed, and the distorted myth of safe sex elevated to a new height of acceptance and credibility. . . .

Where do we find safety in the area of sexual expression? It is found only in abstinence before marriage and monogamy within marriage. This standard allows for sex in the one context where true freedom can exist—a context of love, commitment, and faithfulness.

In the great public debate over sexual conduct that will doubtless continue, the church is obliged to raise again this biblical standard.

Not surprisingly, the message from the New Life pulpit is similarly conservative—its members would say biblical—on morality. Abortion is described as abominable. Homosexuality is a perversion. Preservation of the family is most important; divorce is to be avoided at all costs. Since it is doubtful that many homosexuals call New Life their church home, some of this preaching is clearly a condemnation of the larger society. When asked directly what the important moral issues of the day were, pastor Stone responded that abortion, homosexuality, and traditional gender roles—keeping the family together with the male as head of the household—were the three biggest issues. Stone makes overtures toward "holding people in the church accountable for right action." If members commit adultery, for example, the church has a responsibility to help them see the sinfulness of their ways and, if necessary, to purge them from the flock until they admit their sins, repent, and ask God for forgiveness. Easier said than done. The church's official position is unambiguous, but how are church members held accountable in California's open moral culture?

In fact, there is remarkable variation within New Life regarding morality and its enforcement. After worship services, Jack Hope gives young people morality tracts (published by the Churches of Christ in America in Cookeville, Tennessee) that denounce materialism, divorce, drugs, pornography, alcohol, and violence. For Mike Cooper, greed, adultery, murder, violence on TV, and sexual perversion are the most pervasive evils he sees in the surrounding culture. (Though he has been divorced twice, he didn't name divorce as a sin.) Tom Lang has a broader list: abortion, euthanasia, the existence of poverty and hungry people, the arms race, racial tensions, the environment—in short, things that threaten or demean human life are evil, he believes. Lang's view encompasses moral issues that have exercised the Christian Right in recent years *and* the "social issues" that many in the mainline churches herald in their moral crusades. Richard King is not comfortable with the church's position on abortion and believes it needs to confront racism and sexism in its own midst. While the church clearly leans in a conservative direction, there is no unanimity on many of the controversial moral issues, a circumstance aggravated by the plurality of the community.

The problem for New Life, and all churches, is that they can govern people's lives only if individuals submit to their authority. As Hammond (1992) observes, churches, even conservative evangelical ones, are losing precisely that kind of authority, which was heavily eroded by the cultural revolutions of the 1960s and 1970s. Morality is relative, and people can choose another church if the one they attend ceases to be comfortable. New Life members tend to support a conservative moral agenda—"family values"—but how far the church can go in enforcing its Christian morality is not at all clear. The church discourages divorce, and yet one member complained that he received no support from church leadership in confronting his wife (also a New Life member) who was having an extramarital affair with another member of the congregation.

A specific event focusing on the church's social ministry offers a window onto moral ambiguity at New Life. Evangelical churches are often criticized by liberal churches for their inward focus—their emphasis on personal salvation—at the expense of the service imperative of the Gospel. Pastor Stone is sensitive to this charge and is trying to move the church toward a service ministry for children. That effort was initiated on "Save the Children Sunday," which was held on the second Sunday in February 1992.

During worship on this occasion, two guest speakers shared stories about their ministry with children. One is a missionary in Hong Kong, and the other is the founder and director of a summer camp for physically abused children. "Save the Children Sunday" also dealt with the issue of abortion, which was described as the murder of unborn children. For the first time in several months, the pastor took a strong, explicit position on abortion from the pulpit. He urged the church to get involved with the issue and described abortion as "one of the most horrible sins of our time." To "educate" members on the abortion issue, a video was shown at the Sunday evening gathering that depicted the "abortion industry" as the systematic mutilation of children. Stone suggested that most women who have abortions are selfish and insensitive.

What is most interesting is that the video was shown in a side room on Sunday evening, not in the main hall, and not during or after the morning service. It was made available to people but not forced on them. Church leadership recognizes that there are some differences of opinion among members on the abortion issue. Indeed, I found that the moral terrain at New Life is more complex than stereotypes of Pentecostal churches would suggest, though from the outside members appear uniformly conservative.

I draw three tentative conclusions from my interviews and field observations in two southern churches outside the South. First, displaced southerners *are* among the faithful in southern evangelical churches in California, but they are a minority, and their number is decreasing as the generations pass and the ascriptive power of religious tradition fades. Second, while these southern churches were on the front edge of resurgent evangelicalism, growing rapidly during the 1970s, as aggregate trends indicate, they are no longer vital centers of evangelical faith in the community. In their current poor health they look and act much like mainline churches except that—and this is the third finding—they have a strong oppositional stance toward the surrounding culture, an antimodern public face, which is essentially moral rather than theological resistance. This third factor may limit the attractiveness of these churches and thus contribute to their decline inasmuch as there are evangelical alternatives in the community that are not set against California's secular culture but instead embrace it.

Seen this way, southern religion outside the South does not necessarily represent a fundamental restructuring of American society. Evangelicalism has clearly spread geographically in recent decades, but outside the South there is enormous pressure on it to adapt to the new circumstance if the tradition is to survive. More than changing California, the culture in the West seems to be challenging southern-style religion. That, at least, is what my field work suggests. But aggregate church membership trends show that evangelicalism today is still growing. So if some southern evangelical churches outside the South are struggling, like the two congregations I observed, the next question is what accounts for evangelicalism's continued nationwide growth.

Part III

The Californication
of Conservative Protestantism

CHAPTER FIVE

Resurgent Evangelicalism
and Cultural Accommodation

> Ernst Troeltsch argued that religious relevance is a function
> of achieving in each new historical epoch a compromise be-
> tween the radical teachings of primitive Christianity and the
> culture in which the religion is being practiced. Religious
> institutions that do not change inevitably decline: churches
> that survive and grow will adapt to their culture.
>
> Donald P. Miller

Understanding the spread of southern religion is critical to comprehend-
ing why born-again Christianity is again popular in the waning years of the
twentieth century, but to assess the lasting impact of resurgent evangelicalism,
it is necessary to recognize that growth in southern churches outside the South
may be slowing, and for predictable reasons. Moreover, a new form of
evangelicalism is emerging, one that fits the culture outside the South more
readily than do southern churches. This transformation within evangelicalism,
from prosperous southern churches in the 1950s, '60s, and '70s to prosperous
new forms of evangelicalism today, is a case of religious tradition's adapting to
a changed social context. Some churches adapt more successfully than others,
and there are two such congregations in Central Coast, California, that can be
usefully compared to the New Life Christian Assembly and Hope Baptist
Church.

The Vineyard Christian Fellowship and Calvary Chapel are prototypes of
a rapidly growing new form of evangelical Protestantism in America. They are
nondenominational, born-again Christian organizations that started in beach
communities in Southern California during the 1970s and '80s. They grew up
on the heels of the Jesus movement of the counterculture era, and they em-
body the culture and values of the baby boom generation. These two organizations now have several hundred affiliate churches nationwide and tens of
thousands of devoted members. Participants tend to be young, white, middle-

class, and fairly well educated. A majority of new members came into the fold from other conservative Protestant churches, which is to say they were already born again, but only about one-third were reared in evangelical churches. One-third were raised Catholic, and another third grew up in liberal and moderate Protestant churches (Perrin and Mauss 1991, 102–3).

Members of Vineyard and Calvary Chapel are comfortable with modern life in ways that their counterparts in southern churches are not, and that may explain why New Life and Hope Baptist are struggling congregations while Vineyard and Calvary are flourishing. As Ernst Troeltsch (1976) argued long ago, those churches that survive and grow are those that find ways to accommodate the surrounding culture. When southern churches leave the South, they lose cultural currency. Vineyard and Calvary represent a transformed style of evangelical Protestantism—a reformation of old-time religion—that emerged and is taking root in California's pluralistic soil and is thus more open to contemporary culture.

Religious organizations like Vineyard and Calvary Chapel are innovative and entrepreneurial. They are finding ways to translate a theologically and culturally conservative style of Protestantism into contemporary terms, and they may be growing precisely because they embrace rather than turn against modern culture. That, at least, is the thesis explored in this and the following chapter. It is a story of the *Californication* of conservative Protestantism.

What Is "Contemporary" Evangelicalism?

Participating as an observer in the AGF and SBC congregations required me to wear a coat and tie, standard etiquette in most Protestant churches, both mainline and evangelical, even in Southern California. But, as I discovered, that is inappropriate dress for a Vineyard meeting. If someone strolls in wearing shorts, beach sandals, a T-shirt, and a baseball cap, he or she will be less obtrusive than a suited visitor. Congregants' dress and demeanor are decidedly casual at Vineyard gatherings.

The service at Central Coast's Vineyard opens with thirty minutes of Christian soft rock. Some congregants stand and some sit, but most sing enthusiastically, following the lead of a five-piece electric band. There are no ushers regulating movement during worship; people are free to come and go. This relaxed worship style is surely due to the age of the worshipers—most people in the congregation are baby boomers—but it may also have to do with region; this is a version of evangelicalism that accommodates to California's laid-back culture.

The Vineyard style of worship—the blending of evangelical Protestant belief with elements of contemporary culture—is reminiscent of a metaphor used by Catherine Albanese (1988). She invokes an image of California as a "Phoenix grave"—a region in which the traditional cultures of its immigrant populations break down, mix, and ferment. From the rubble emerges a new, uniquely American culture. In her image, therefore, evangelicalism outside the South gradually loses its southernness if it is to prosper. That is a plausible way to understand the emergence of new evangelical forms like the Vineyard, and if it is accurate, two new research questions can be asked. First, are there people who started in a southern church and then switched to a new-style evangelical congregation? And second, are there southern churches thriving in the 1990s outside the South because they made the necessary accommodations? A tentative answer to both questions is yes, but a fuller answer must await future research.

So what is "accommodative" or "contemporary" evangelicalism? Here the self-understanding of the new evangelical leadership is useful. In a Vineyard publication called *Signs and Wonders Today,* John Wimber, founder of the Vineyard Christian Fellowship, observes that the prewar generation

> is beginning to pass from the evangelical church scene without replacing itself. Few churches are effectively reaching the young—those who do not feel comfortable with the lifestyle, music or jargon of establishment Christianity. We are reaching them. As a young church, we experience all of the opportunities and problems which accompany youth. Our young 18 to 25 year old attenders are providing the spiritual dynamic which enables us to reach out to a young culture and relate the Gospel to them. Because we are young, we are current. We speak the language of these people. Our sermons and songs are familiar and acceptable. We find ourselves communicating eternal truths in a contemporary style. . . . Many people have chosen to opt out of the religious system because they felt they couldn't live up to the standards the church set for them. Others have been battered and burned by well meaning, but harsh, treatment. Cultural differences have made it difficult for others to relate to the traditional church. Many of these religious refugees are finding us. (1990, 19)

A "contemporary" evangelical church, then, is nondenominational and is not antagonistic to the surrounding culture, a fundamentally secular and youth-oriented milieu. Vineyard and Calvary are two such churches, and that may help explain why they and not their southern evangelical counterparts are healthy and growing in Central Coast, California. A short anecdote will help illustrate the new evangelicals' comfort with secular culture.

The setting was a Halloween costume party in October 1992 in an upper-middle-class neighborhood. The guests were mostly professionals in their thirties and forties. They were college educated; some had children; most were members of two-income families; few were California natives. The hosts, recent migrants from New England, had no church affiliation. If anything, they were antagonistic toward organized religion. Midway through the evening, two women and two men congregated for conversation on a backyard patio. These guests knew each other, though they had come to the party separately. Three of the four were smoking cigarettes, and all were drinking alcohol, either beer or a heavily spiked Halloween punch. One of the men steered the conversation in a bawdy direction, and for perhaps thirty minutes they laughed and exchanged dirty jokes. There is nothing unusual about smoking, drinking, and telling colorful stories at a party, but, it turns out, all four people in the conversation were born-again Christians—adult converts—and they all attended Calvary Chapel. These Calvary members were indulging in behavior that would be condemned as sinful in more traditional evangelical settings. Indeed, New Life Christian Assembly, fearing the evil connotations even of a Halloween celebration, hosted an alternative Christian party in their church basement on Halloween night.

Eventually the conversation turned to a church picnic fundraiser all four people had attended earlier that day, and it was clear from the talk that they take their church involvement seriously; they are not merely Sunday morning Christians. When asked what was appealing about the church, one of the woman replied simply and without hesitation, "They preach the truth." The truth of salvation through Jesus Christ, she meant, as revealed in the Bible. Theologically, she sounded like a fundamentalist, but she is a worldly women—a well-paid professional, twice married, articulate, supremely self-confident, and perfectly comfortable in the secular world of a yuppie Halloween party.

This is only one story, but it illustrates the degree to which some evangelical churches accommodate to and tolerate lifestyle choices that would be unthinkable in a more traditional context. It is hard to imagine encountering Hope Baptist or New Life members in this setting. Social and cultural norms at the Vineyard and Calvary Chapel are simply different from those I found in the two southern churches in that they accommodate to much of the secular world that envelops their church membership in California.

Church Growth and Cultural Accommodation

The Vineyard Christian Fellowship in this community was established in 1986. For several years it met for Sunday worship in a movie theater, but it has changed worship sites every few years because the congregation is growing so rapidly. It currently meets in a vacant warehouse, averaging three to four hundred people for the Sunday meeting, but "home groups" are more important to members than the Sunday morning worship service. These groups are composed of members with common interests and concerns who come together to study the Bible, pray, and support each other. The meetings occur in members' homes or other settings outside the church. "This is where people really get their needs met," the church receptionist says. She is a thirty-something native Californian who has attended Vineyard meetings for several years and is very enthusiastic about the church. She describes herself as a "Bapta-Presby-Methopalian," someone who has been all over the religious map. Vineyard is attractive to her because of its nonhierarchical, participatory style. "I'm very comfortable here," she says. "The pastor isn't like a dictator. He has a soft voice and a very casual way. He isn't shaking his finger at us and condemning people." When asked if she was happy at Vineyard, she said, "Yes, I think its good for right now." This seems a rather noncommittal response for someone so excited about a church, but that is the nature of membership among baby boomers; their organizational commitments are more tenuous than those of their parents' generation (see Roof 1993).

The Calvary Chapel congregation in Central Coast was established in 1976 and met at the local YMCA for almost twelve years. The congregation grew consistently during that time, with as many as 800 adults calling Calvary their home church. In 1988 the congregation divided over pastoral leadership and attendance dropped to between 200 and 300. In 1989 the church bought property on the edge of town, not far from New Life and Hope Baptist, and it is again growing rapidly, beyond the capacity of its new facilities. With nearly 1,000 current members, including 250 children in Sunday school, Calvary was having three worship services on Sunday and thus decided to rent space for morning worship in the city's largest downtown theater, which accommodates its numbers.

Calvary's office receptionist is also thirty-something and is a five-year member. She came to Calvary from a Lutheran church but was raised Catholic. When asked why Calvary seems to be growing so rapidly, she responded, "Because we teach right from the Bible, but our services aren't liturgical, and we have lots of programs and activities." Then she added, "But I really think its the Lord's work." The Calvary and Vineyard congregations in Central Coast are clearly growing, and it may be because they are more open than old-line evangelicals to diverse lifestyle choices prevalent in California.

Scholarly attention to growing churches like Vineyard and Calvary Chapel is new. In one of the few published studies on Vineyard, Robin D. Perrin and Armand L. Mauss (1991, 105) contend that people join in part because they perceive the Vineyard to be more "serious" about religion than their previous church communities. Using measures of commitment, discipline, and mission-

ary zeal, Perrin and Mauss's finding tends to support the Kelley thesis that evangelical churches are growing because they are more "strict" than other churches,
though their measures may tap strength of commitment more than strictness.
No doubt Vineyard members are strongly committed to the church, to its leadership, and to sharing their Christian faith, but that does not necessarily mean
these are strict churches theologically or morally. In fact, they do not exhibit
the cultural rigidity found in churches like Hope Baptist and New Life. Vineyard and Calvary members may be highly committed, but they are *not* cultural
conservatives in several important ways.

Donald P. Miller and his colleagues at the University of Southern California have undertaken the most comprehensive study to date of the new-style
evangelicalism (that is, the style seen in churches like Vineyard and Calvary) and
call the churches that practice it "rapidly growing nonmainline churches." They
report that these nonmainline churches are growing because of innovations allowing them to accommodate the cultural preferences of the baby boom generation, preferences that are anti-institutional, informal, nondogmatic, therapeutic,
and more tolerant of alternative lifestyles than established churches. (Miller and
Kennedy 1991) Their findings are antithetical to the Kelley thesis and the Perrin
and Mauss findings. Their research suggests that perhaps tolerance, not strictness, accounts for the prosperity of these new evangelical organizations.

More specifically, Miller argues that these churches are "culturally current," that they look and feel like other contemporary social institutions rather
than established churches or sectarian religious organizations standing in opposition to secular culture. Put differently, not only are these churches *in* the
modern world, they are *of* the modern world. Vineyard and Calvary, and
churches like them, distance themselves from established religion by accom-
modating the cultural preferences of young people whose values and lifestyle
choices have been shaped directly or indirectly by the social upheavals of the
1960s and 1970s. The worship settings in these churches contain no overt
Christian symbols, no chancel choir, no lectern for preaching, and no altar—
just a stage with microphones and amplified musical instruments. The pastor is
relaxed and conversational in preaching, as though talking to friends. In the
following passage, Miller describes the cultural currency he encountered in
one setting:

> At the most basic physical level, Hope Chapel disassociates itself from
> institutional religious forms that baby boomers and teenagers tend to
> reject. Traditional religion is deemed to be bureaucratic and authoritar-
> ian, and thereby alienating. To accommodate this perception, the meet-
> ing places and buildings . . . do not look like conventional churches.

They are highly utilitarian spaces which lack steeples, stained glass, or other religious symbols. Likewise, clergy avoid the appearance of religious professionals, by wearing casual clothes rather than vestments or clerical collars. The very absence of "sacred space" appears to locate the sacred in the internal experience of the people. Likewise, the pastoral staff does not serve as the mediator between God and man; rather, there is an affirmation of the priesthood of all believers. In Weberian terms, authority is charismatic and prophetic, rather than bureaucratic or traditional. . . . Going to church is no more intimidating than attending a rock concert or going to the local shopping mall. There is no need to worry about what to wear or how to act. Everyone seems to be accepted on his or her own terms. Indeed, there seems to be an invitation "to be yourself." (1992, 9–10)

This description is consistent with the worship setting and experience I encountered in both the Vineyard and Calvary congregations in Central Coast, California, and this currency seems critical to their popularity.

Miller cautions that while currency may be essential for growth, it is not a complete explanation of it. He cites the ability of nonmainline churches to mediate profound religious experience for their members as another, and perhaps more critical, factor for understanding growth (1992, 12). No doubt successful religious organizations successfully mediate religious experience for members, but emphasizing the mediation of experience in explaining growth and decline runs the risk of underestimating the significance of the fit between the form of religious experience and acceptable forms of behavior in the wider culture. If religious institutions are fundamentally social, as I argue, then cultural form is paramount in understanding growth and decline.

The two southern evangelical churches I visited are mediating deeply felt religious experience for their members, but neither is growing. Why? Hope Baptist and New Life represent an old style of evangelical Protestantism—one linked to southern culture—with which many young people, particularly outside the South, have no affinity. It is *because* they blend in with other contemporary forms of social life that Vineyard and Calvary successfully recruit religious seekers in California. My assumption is that all churches in some way mediate religious experience. The important sociological questions therefore are what cultural form it takes, what form fits in where geographically, and with whom certain forms are popular. The new-style evangelicalism is attractive to southern Californians and young people generally in ways that the religion of the Old South is not. An examination of the position of new-style churches on theological and moral issues helps to clarify this difference.

The New Evangelical Morality

Calvary Chapel emphasizes the literal interpretation of the Bible and in that sense could be called fundamentalist, but parishioners would be uncomfortable with that label. Certainly they are not reacting to secular culture in the oppositional way that early-twentieth-century fundamentalists did. The same is true for Vineyard. These evangelical Christians are more charismatic than fundamentalist, but their worship experience involves personal prophecy more than the righteous word of God revealed in tongues, a phenomenon associated with early Pentecostalism. The religious culture in these congregations, mirroring the direction of change in the wider culture, is more individualistic and therapeutic than social and moralistic. "Vineyard members express . . . [themselves] at individual rather than at structural levels," Miller and Kennedy observe. "Solving the turmoil of marriages, being a responsible parent, and loving the neighbor next door are difficult enough tasks without feeling the burden to eliminate war or solve third world hunger" (1991, 17). One wonders, then, if the opposition to abortion and other "family values" issues paramount in old-line evangelical communities and among other cultural conservatives are not also secondary to the specific needs of individuals. If so, the relative vitality of new evangelicalism compared to southern religion has important implications for understanding how resurgent evangelicalism is affecting America's so-called culture war. Born-again Christianity may be more changed by society than it changes society.

Ninety-five percent of those surveyed by Miller are born-again Christians, but only 37 percent say that the Bible is to be understood as the "actual word of God." Most others say that it is the "inspired word of God" (1992, 14–15). And they place a high premium on sharing the faith. Thus these Christians are a new type of evangelical, theologically conservative but not cultural traditionalists, clearly related to southern religion but not antagonistic toward the modern scientific worldview. An even larger difference, however, between old and new evangelicalism is found on social issues, adherents' views toward the wider culture. Paul Kennedy's Vineyard study (1992) turned up some remarkable findings in this regard. He concludes that "those attending the Vineyard Anaheim are quite liberal with respect to civil liberties, racial justice, and some measures of women's rights—except for abortion. [But] with respect to moral and sexual issues, the Vineyard is much more conservative than other denominations" (1992, 7).

Miller says that the teachings in these churches are unambiguous, a claim consistent with the notion that the churches are growing because they are "serious." While they may be *theologically* unambiguous, in my experience they are more tolerant of alternative lifestyles than the teachings of old-line evangelicals, to whom moral issues are not unambiguous. Furthermore, preaching in Vineyard or Calvary services lacks the judgmental moral tone of preaching in the southern churches. While the Vineyard may be conservative on issues of sexual morality, as Kennedy reports, it and churches like it do not condemn. In fact, Calvary Chapel's minister recently married a lesbian couple, an unthinkable event for both southern churches in this study. There seems to be a functional if not ideological tolerance for alternative lifestyles. The "prolife" agenda, for instance, is a "ministry" that people can choose to participate in, like a singles group, a golfing club, mission work, a Bible study, or a surfing group. Participation in these groups is by choice; church members are not obliged to be "prolife" to be in good standing in the community.

In summary, what is important about this new form of evangelicalism is its fit with contemporary culture, its growing comfort with a pluralistic world. No doubt this fit is a result of age and migration from country to city, but it is also fundamentally related to geographic region. The Vineyard Christian Fellowship and Calvary Chapel, in fact, started in California, though they are growing nationally. If my secondary thesis is correct, however—that churches cannot survive in the long run unless they accommodate their surroundings—then the new evangelicals may have limited success in planting churches in the South, for example, unless they do so in urban areas where the social conditions that spawned this evangelical form in California are also far advanced. This issue is explored in the next chapter.

My point here is not to argue that new-style evangelicalism is uniquely Californian. There are nondenominational evangelical churches in other regions of the country, such as Willow Creek Community Church outside Chicago, that embrace rather than resist contemporary culture and are thus growing. It happens, however, that several of the important organizations comprising this movement are native to California, and that should not be surprising. Religious innovation typically comes on the cultural fringe, where it is least suppressed by the religious establishment, and California is part of the least churched region of the country (see Hammond 1992 and Shibley 1992). It is also part of the most culturally pluralistic and therefore most religiously "open" region (Stark and Bainbridge 1985).

Why is it important whether resurgent evangelicalism is southern or nonsouthern, old or new? It is important for the simple reason that new-style evangelicalism, nonsouthern, is more tolerant of contemporary lifestyles. Indeed, it is a product of contemporary culture. If southern-style religion is sweeping the nation and taking root, then perhaps American culture is shifting to the right ideologically. But if southern churches are being transformed outside the South, if they must accommodate to survive, then perhaps restructuring theses that confound evangelical growth and cultural conservatism (see Wuthnow 1988 and Hunter 1991) misinterpret the meaning of religious and cultural change in contemporary America. A careful look inside a Vineyard congregation in a major metropolitan area in the midwest is revealing in this regard. It allows an examination of the viability of Vineyard-style evangelicalism outside California, and if resurgent evangelicalism in the heartland celebrates rather than condemns popular culture, then the spread of new religious organizations like the Vineyard and Calvary Chapel may indeed signal the Californication of conservative Protestantism in American.

CHAPTER SIX

Jesus Rocks
Portrait of a Vibrant Vineyard Congregation

It's not until a disk jockey from the . . . all-Christian radio
station mounts the pulpit and asks, "How excited are you
about Jesus Christ?" that the place explodes. At once everyone is flowing into the aisles, stomping, clapping and shriek-
ing. The whole church is suddenly wired, keening with the
sort of thrilled excitation that you find, well, at a rock concert. Which, suddenly, this Friday night service has become.
Four pretty young women with microphones sweep onto the
altar. A soundtrack pulsing with synthesizers, drum machines
and a horn section begins blasting loud and hard.

Nicholas Dawidoff

Midwest Vineyard, which meets in a public high school auditorium on
Sunday morning, is part of a nationwide movement numbering more than three
hundred congregations.[1] It is a middle-class suburban assembly, largely white
but with some racial diversity. Slightly more women then men attend regularly, and people are casually dressed, as if to go shopping at the mall, out for
pizza, or to walk the dog. Most are in their twenties or thirties. There is more
faded denim in the auditorium than any other fabric, few women wear dresses,
Birkenstocks are plentiful, and scarcely any gray hair is visible. This is clearly a
youthful crowd. While the 900-seat auditorium is never quite full on Sunday
morning, there is a consistently large and energetic group. These congregants
come to praise God and do so with abundant spirit. They are the next generation of born-again Christians. But there is a paradox here: Vineyard members
are theologically conservative and world-affirming; they are culturally hip
evangelicals.

In the twentieth century, evangelical Protestants have more or less set
themselves apart from the secular world, retreating into a subculture that defined liberalism and other modern values as corrosive of Christian life. This is,

---

1. Midwest Vineyard is a pseudonym.

in fact, the social and cultural meaning of Protestant fundamentalism (see Ammerman 1987). Moreover, evangelicals have tended to subscribe to a premillennial theology that focused their attention on otherworldly affairs and often led them to condemn earthly pursuits and pleasures—rock and roll music, for example—as the work of the devil. In short, evangelical Protestants have been preeminently concerned with establishing and maintaining boundaries between themselves and the rest of the world. Boundaries change, however, and Midwest Vineyard illustrates the permeability of cultural barriers between religions and the wider society.

Consider this extended excerpt from field notes covering my three months of field work at Midwest Vineyard:

Worship this morning seemed more like a rock concert than a religious gathering. Perhaps the two aren't that different sociologically. This church cultivates a style of worship that is compatible with youth culture.

I arrived a few minutes late, about 10:40, and passed a young Asian man (college age) in the long hallway leading to the auditorium. He was leaning against the cement wall near the men's room, one hand in his pocket and the other gripping a portable phone. He was smiling and engaged in a casual phone conversation. The service had already started, but people seem to come and go as they please.

When I entered the auditorium, the band on stage (the "worship team") was playing upbeat music, and a gathering of close to 600 people stood clapping, swaying to the beat, and singing enthusiastically. The volume was high though not uncomfortable. The band, as usual, was a seven-piece ensemble: two guitars (one acoustic, one electric), an electric bass, drums, an electric keyboard and synthesizer, and two backup vocalists. The five instrumentalists, including the worship leader, were men. Most wore jeans and cotton pullover shirts; one wore a T-shirt that said, "Jesus Rocks." The two singers were women. One wore black spandex tights, the other slacks. The sound quality was high, the performance professional. Three sound wizards, all men, one with shoulder-length hair, sat behind a massive sound board in the middle of the auditorium. They were mixing and recording the service.

I took a seat in the middle of the room, first row of the second section, adjacent to the sound engineers. Most of the crowd was in front of me, careening toward the stage. In fact, few seats were still available up front—remarkable for a Protestant worship service, in my experience.

(In "mainline" churches, back-row pews often fill first.) But this was a lively and earnest crowd—spirit-filled, it would describe itself. The congregation is young and eager.

It is a come-as-you-are gathering. Anyone is welcome, it seems. There was a woman behind me nursing her infant; she was otherwise alone. Lots of single men and women attend these services. A few minutes after I arrived, several people in their twenties walked in and took seats in front of me. One of the young women was dressed in black tights, miniskirt, lace top, and studded leather jacket. She had dyed hair and a pierced nose. Her outfit was striking, but her presence drew no special attention. Several rows in front of her stood a man I've noticed for several weeks. He wears tie-dye more often than not, has a mohawk haircut (this week his hair is dyed green), and wears a small silver cross earring in his pierced right ear. He looks about thirty. Several others wore tie-dye; it isn't typical, but it's not unusual. Lots of men had long hair, some in ponytails. Some men wore slacks with button-down Oxford shirts and had short, well combed hair, but none of them wore a tie.

While worship is almost always accompanied by amplified instrumental music, the music is often melancholic—Christian soft rock—though it can be quite celebratory. Today the congregation seemed especially lively, and the musicians, feeding off the excitement, played one upbeat song after another, running on perhaps ten minutes longer than usual. The music portion of worship crescendoed over thirty minutes and culminated in a fevered pitch with people jumping, dancing in place, and waving their hands in the air. When the music finally ended, the congregation remained standing and broke into applause; they clapped, shouted, and whistled, as if calling for an encore. The musicians looked pleased, and the pastor who came on stage to make announcements backed off and allowed the band to play another song. The excitement was completely spontaneous, and at that moment, in the midst of that youthful crowd, the worship service seemed a lot like a rock concert. (field notes, March 27, 1994)

Compared to the style of Baptists in the South and Southern Baptists in California, Midwest Vineyard's new style of evangelical worship represents movement toward popular culture and thus a redefinition of what is acceptable and what is deviant behavior in conservative Protestant circles. Groups like the Vineyard are on the front edge of evangelical Protestant accommodation to the wider culture.

Midwest Vineyard and the Movement

The Vineyard movement is designed to appeal to a generation of young people disillusioned with traditional institutions, including religion. One of Midwest's pastors joked one Sunday morning about having psychedelic posters of Jesus on the walls of his college dorm room in the early 1970s, and this reminiscence resonated with his parishioners.

The Vineyard movement draws primarily on white middle-class baby boomers. Churches in the movement emphasize healing, prophecy, and other gifts of the Holy Spirit. In this way they differ from Calvary Chapel, which is not charismatic, but culturally and demographically the two movements are similar. As noted above, these churches have the following organizational and cultural characteristics. They

(1) are adverse to established, institutional forms of religion;

(2) have a democratic structure of religious authority;

(3) stress religious experience rather than theological dogma;

(4) have therapeutic values and a tolerance for individual differences but are devoid of moral relativism;

(5) are program oriented. (Miller and Kennedy 1991)

All of these features are present in Midwest Vineyard, though this congregation has a history independent from the early Vineyard movement in California.

Midwest Vineyard started in 1976 as a nondenominational fellowship of about 40 people. As one brochure recounting the church's history states, "The founders of the church experienced the power of God in the charismatic renewal of the late sixties and early seventies, and were yearning for a church that would place a high priority on *contemporary* worship, biblical teaching, openness to the Holy Spirit, and committed relationship" (emphasis added). The social conditions that spawned this Midwest congregation are the same ones that gave birth to religious innovation in California in the 1960s and '70s. Some of the founders were baby boomers reared in conservative Protestant churches who wanted to escape denominational structures and outdated traditions. Hence congregational structure was very decentralized in Midwest's early years. By 1980, membership at Midwest Vineyard stagnated at 150–200, and thus the church sought a "renewed renewal" of the Holy Spirit in its midst. Through the ministry of John Wimber and the Vineyard movement, it came into the Association of Vineyard Churches in 1984. Today about 700 adults attend Midwest Vineyard regularly.

A self-conducted survey of the congregation in 1992 provides a telling demographic profile of Midwest Vineyard congregants.

There were no survey items on race, but my Sunday morning observations suggest that perhaps 20 percent of the congregation is nonwhite (mostly African American and Asian American), mirroring the wider community. No racial minorities play significant leadership roles during the worship service, but an African American male was recently hired to direct the Urban Ministry Program. An African American woman serves as the associate pastor for children. More women attend Midwest Vineyard than men (56 percent to 44 percent), but men dominate leadership positions. The Sunday program and other church literature lists husband-and-wife teams on the pastoral staff in the following way: "Tom and Lisa Johnson, Senior Pastor" or "Paul and Kim Lucas, Executive Pastor." Tom and Paul lead Sunday worship; Lisa and Kim are not involved in the service. In fact, no women are in leadership roles during Sunday worship, only in supporting roles such as serving communion, sharing a vision, or performing music or dance. Lisa Johnson, however, is coordinator of the women's ministry, and Kim Lucas, as director of counseling services, coordinates an eight-person staff. Church staff composition and leadership responsibilities during worship suggest that Midwest Vineyard maintains traditional gender roles, though less rigidly than most conservative Protestant congregations.

These observations are consistent with what Paul Kennedy (1992) found in his Vineyard study, but Midwest Vineyard appears to be even younger than the typical Vineyard congregation. The average age at Midwest Vineyard is thirty-one, and 83 percent of its members are under the age of forty, which suggests that this is a young boomer, even postboomer, crowd. Remarkably, 63 percent of Midwest Vineyard members are college-educated. No doubt this is related to the church's close proximity to a major midwestern university. Kennedy reports that 46 percent of the congregants at the Anaheim Vineyard, the movement's home base, have college degrees (1992, 2).

These numbers are astonishing when compared to Hunter's earlier findings on the demographic characteristics of liberal Protestants and evangelicals generally. He reported in *American Evangelicalism* that the average age of liberal Protestants is forty-five, and forty-eight is the average age of evangelicals. He also found that only 14 percent of liberal Protestants and 9 percent of evangelicals have college degrees (1983, 50–54). Certainly those figures have risen since Hunter's study, but even so, there appears to be a large difference in educational attainment between old-line Protestants, both liberal and conservative, and the new evangelicals. Twenty-two percent of Midwest Vineyard members have graduate degrees. By comparison, a recent survey of Presbyterians shows that 20 percent of their membership nationally have graduate degrees (Presbyterian Panel 1993). There is no measure of income for the Midwest congregation, but Kennedy reports that 54 percent of the Anaheim Vineyard has an annual family income of $40,000 or more; many are professionals.

The Vineyard movement challenges the old stereotype that evangelical Protestants are not well educated and have lower economic status than other religious groups. Evangelical Protestantism was identified by H. Richard Niebuhr (1965) as a "church of the disinherited," and born-again Christians have been struggling for decades to enter the socioeconomic and cultural mainstream of American society (see Marsden 1987). They have succeeded with the emergence of new evangelical churches like the Vineyard. But acceptance into the cultural mainstream has costs, and one of those appears to be the loosening of the moral boundaries that have historically separated evangelicals from other Christians and non-Christians.

Vineyard Beliefs and Practices

It is possible that what I see as liberalism in Vineyard congregations is a surface phenomenon. It matters little whether or not evangelicals wear jeans instead of polyester and listen to rock and roll instead of country music if these behaviors are not connected to liberal values. The Halloween party described in the previous chapter, however, suggests that cultural accommodation among new-style evangelicals runs much deeper than clothing styles and musical tastes. But that was in California. What does the new evangelicalism look like in a more conservative Midwest setting?

Sunday worship is a primary site for the expression of a group's beliefs and practices in relation to the sacred, and Midwest Vineyard's morning celebrations reveal plainly the breadth and depth of cultural liberalism among the new-style evangelicals in this congregation. What do Vineyard members believe? How do they express their faith? Is Vineyard belief and practice similar to or different from other forms of evangelicalism? The following comments are based on direct observations of Sunday worship and on material in church publications that are available during and after the services.

Most important for Vineyard members, Christian faith is profoundly personal and Jesus-centered; they are born-again Christians striving for intimacy with their God. When individuals commit their lives to Jesus Christ as adults, they believe, His spirit comes into their hearts and causes a "new birth." The Vineyard orientation packet for new and potential members includes publications by Inter-Varsity Christian Fellowship and the International Church of the Foursquare Gospel that emphasize the importance of a personal relationship with Jesus, animated by the Holy Spirit. The thirty to forty minutes of "worship" that opens each Sunday service is at once a celebration of that relationship and a yearning of congregants to deepen their connection to God by being open to the power of the Holy Spirit. This portion of Sunday service is sometimes solemn and sometimes festive, but it is always heartfelt. Virtually everyone in attendance is involved in worship, actively praying to Jesus or singing His praise.

Along with the acceptance of Jesus Christ as lord and savior and the subsequent spiritual rebirth, an important element of belief and practice among Vineyard members is their use of scripture. The Bible is referred to often and with deference during the service. The church's formal statement of faith says that its adherents "believe in the Bible as the inspired Word of God, without error, and the final authority of Christian life and faith." Elsewhere in church literature the Bible is referred to as the "infallible rule of faith and practice." The Bible (many people carry the New International Version) is the authoritative word of God, and scripture is typically quoted during the service as "proof" of some position or another. In a "teaching" (a conversational sermon) one Sunday on the role of emotions in Christian life, for example, the senior pastor said, "God is emotional," and then quoted Psalms 78:40, 58 and Luke 15:20 to substantiate the claim. He followed this with the statement "God desires passionate relations with others" and then quoted Romans 11:12 and Revelation 3:15–20 and 2:4–5 as proof of his assertion. A typical teaching may last forty-five minutes and make reference to two or three dozen specific passages from scripture, all used to bolster the speaker's claims. The scriptures used in the teachings are shown by overhead projector on the auditorium screen behind the stage and are thus visible to everyone in the room. This is done despite the fact that perhaps half of those in attendance are carrying Bibles with dog-eared pages and underlined passages.

A third essential feature of Vineyard belief and practice is commitment to sharing the faith. Along with attending worship celebrations, members are expected to be involved in some form of ministry to others. Every Sunday service is punctuated with testimony about the Vineyard's "ministry"—the rhetoric of evangelistic work. Discussion topics may include plans to "plant" churches in other midwestern cities, the struggles of newly founded congregations (two churches were planted in 1993, one in Dublin, Ireland, and the other in a midwestern United States suburb), missionary work overseas, local urban and student ministry, and a Vineyard-inspired charismatic revival in England. The Vineyard movement is growth oriented, always focused on starting new ministries. Midwest Vineyard's size and the rapid growth of the movement as a whole testify to the success of the movement's evangelistic work. However, contrary to stereotypes of zealous Christian evangelists, these evangelical Protestants soft-sell their faith with a nonconfrontational style. Their work is earnest, but Vineyard members are as committed to serving others as they are to converting others; they not only save souls for the afterlife but also take care of bodies in this life; their evangelistic disposition is more dialogue than monologue.

The quantity and quality of overseas mission work offer a striking example of Midwest Vineyard's evangelistic impulse. A missions brochure claims that in the past six years, more than 250 people from this congregation have served in short-term missions (in Australia, Austria, Ecuador, Egypt, England, Haiti, India, Ireland, Japan, Kenya, Latvia, Mexico, Poland, Scotland, South Africa, Spain, Sweden, Thailand, and Turkey).

In particular, two overseas mission ventures sponsored by Midwest Vineyard reveal a range in the quality of work being done. The Turkey Project is an effort to help Christianize the non-Christian world. A Midwest Vineyard couple in their thirties will be moving to Turkey to assist in a long-term ministry to introduce Muslims to Christianity. In a Sunday morning testimonial calling for financial and spiritual support, the couple told the congregation that "over 99 percent of Turks are Muslim, and the entire country has fewer than five hundred Christian converts from a Muslim background. Yet Turkey is also one of the most open Muslim countries in the world to Christian witness, for the secular constitution guarantees freedom of religious belief. There are no anticonversion laws in the country. Many observers see the next ten years as crucial to the evangelization of the country since the doors are currently open" (field notes, February 13, 1994). While this seems like a traditional evangelical outlook (and may be offensive to liberal Christians who believe there are many paths to heaven), the strategy is to support the growth of an "indigenous" church through the development of local leaders rather than trying to convert individual Muslims at random through an itinerant ministry. Vineyard's mission literature stresses the need to "send people at the request of the local church. Those sent will be qualified to meet specific needs, and will go as servants of the local leadership." The Turkey-bound missionaries talked at length about their need to learn the native language and study Muslim culture to be effective. The goal of conversion is clear, but the method is soft-sell, even dialogical. The man of the team has a divinity degree and a longstanding ministry vocation, and the woman's background is in nutritional education.

Midwest Vineyard also supports two missionaries in Guatemala, a couple also in their early thirties who, in their picture posted on the Mission Work board outside the auditorium, look like Peace Corps volunteers or flower children. Their work in Guatemala focuses on technical aid and service to rural communities. The blurb on their project describes the development of rudimentary irrigation systems to help rural farmers water their crops and the cultivation of native herbs for medicinal use. The emphasis is on "appropriate technology." There is no mention of converting non-Christians. Most of the mission projects supported by Midwest Vineyard are somewhere between the conversion and service paradigms represented by the projects in Turkey and Guatemala respectively.

In summary, Vineyard beliefs and practices affirm traditional evangelical doctrine: Midwest members are born again, they view scripture as authoritative, and they actively share the good news of salvation in Jesus Christ. Yet Vineyard members are not "Bible believers" in the conventional sense. One teaching in a month-long series on emotions explicitly criticized some evangelical Protestants' preoccupation with doctrine and the fundamentalist impulse to pull away from society. Christians ought to be passionate about faith and engaged in the world, the pastor said. They ought to emulate the work of Jesus: feed the hungry, clothe the naked, and heal the sick (field notes, February 13, 1994). Vineyard pastors talk about the imminent return of Christ, but the premillennial theology of traditional evangelicals is considerably relaxed in this congregation. Its commitment to serve others in the community even suggests a postmillennial outlook—an optimism about the perfectibility of society. While these new evangelicals certainly resemble their conservative Protestant forebears and southern evangelical counterparts, their worldly turn indicates a new relationship between evangelicals and the wider culture.

Midwest Vineyard's Expanded Moral Universe

It is clear from a review of Midwest belief and practice that Vineyard members are theologically conservative Protestants, but what about their views on social issues? And how do they behave? Where do they fall on the tolerance-for-diversity continuum represented by the Southern Baptist and Calvary Chapel positions on homosexuality discussed in the previous chapter? In other words, does their theological conservatism extend to social issues? Or is the Vineyard quite liberal on many important social issues, as Kennedy found in his research? Again, the Sunday morning gathering is a window onto answers to these questions.

The metropolitan area adjacent to Midwest Vineyard's suburban community is largely segregated racially, though there are pockets of diversity, and churches are among the most segregated institutions within the community, as they are in most places. Against this backdrop, Midwest Vineyard is a relatively integrated and open congregation, perhaps because it is not tied to denominational and regional histories troubled by racial tension. A number of mixed-race couples attend Midwest Vineyard regularly, and while race and ethnic minorities are not routinely involved in leadership during worship, two important staff positions are now filled by African Americans. On Palm Sunday the fifth- and sixth-grade classes paraded around the auditorium with palm leaves during worship. Of the twenty children participating, two were African American, four were of Asian descent, and the rest were Caucasian. This distribution is close to the racial composition of the congregation as a whole. Accompanying this racial mix is a distinctly liberal view of race issues.

Midwest Vineyard's senior pastor, Tom Johnson, gave a sermon in the spring of 1992 in response to the riots in Los Angeles that followed the verdict in the Rodney King case. His message was adapted and published as a pamphlet that is available at the literature table following worship; it is called "A Biblical Response to the American Racial Crisis." The document sharply condemns violence as a solution to social problems, but it is an unambiguously liberal view of race issues in the United States. The pastor wrote,

> In the wake of the riots in Los Angeles I began to prayerfully study the Bible, looking for a Biblical response to the situation. I knew that the Bible had hundreds of scriptures about the poor and the importance of ministering to them, but I never suspected it had so much to say about the problems of a multi-ethnic society. I found dozens of scriptures that spoke very directly to the ethnic problems we are struggling with so much. The result is that I have become convinced that God has a plan for a multi-ethnic society—something other than what we are experiencing.

The document outlines seven steps necessary to achieve multi-ethnic peace, each supported by two or three scripture references. They are as follows.

(1) Legal equality—have the same laws for everyone.

(2) Equal justice—governmental authority is to be used fairly and equitably.

(3) Provide for the poor—don't allow ethnic minorities to suffer under poverty.

(4) Give minorities a share in ownership—a piece of the pie.

(5) Cultivate sensitivity to the feelings of minorities/other ethnic groups.

(6) Allow no toleration of personal prejudice or mistreatment of ethnic minorities.

(7) Deal with the heart problems of ethnic divisions (e.g., stereotypes, fears, suspicions, judgments, bitterness, hatred).

The race document avoids advocating political action on, for instance, civil rights issues or welfare reform. Rather the pastor's concern is with his Vineyard congregation and whether or not its members are working toward these goals in their own lives. He says that so far in our history, "most of the Church has simply reflected the divisions in society. Even many so called 'social action churches' [that is, of the liberal Protestant mainline churches] are committed to political action but are not actually living a vital example of multi-ethnic people living, working together, understanding and loving each other" (teaching pamphlet, June 7, 1992).

Johnson is correct in saying that the many so-called liberal denominations often do not themselves model the multicultural ethic they advocate in policy statements. According to a recent survey, the Presbyterian church, which gave controversial support to Angela Davis's legal defense fund in the 1960s, is today 98 percent white in membership. Kennedy's study of the Anaheim Vineyard found, remarkably, that 96 percent of the members surveyed opposed laws against interracial marriages (1992, 7). By comparison, Roof and McKinney found that only 73 percent of liberal Protestants and 42 percent of conservative Protestants oppose laws against interracial marriages (1987, 198–99).

Midwest Vineyard is similarly liberal on class issues. Service to the poor is an ethic referred to often during Sunday services, though this is a solidly middle-class congregation. One of the pastor's teachings admonished the congregation to "work to serve the poor and the cause of justice, not as 'political animals,' but as servants of Christ" (teaching pamphlet, June 7, 1992). The message from Midwest leaders is not radical, but the Vineyard ethic is clearly liberal on race and class issues, espousing service to those less fortunate and justice for the oppressed.

Vineyard members tend to be conservative about sexuality, abortion, and gender roles—that constellation of issues the Christian Right has labeled family values. Yet the most striking thing about these issues at Midwest Vineyard is that they are *not* prominently featured in congregational life. Vineyard has a variety of programs designed to support families generally (for example, premarital and postmarital counseling, house groups for new mothers, and family retreats), but there is no reactionary political program associated with its family ministries. These issues as political issues simply do not occupy center stage in congregational life. By contrast, "family values" as political issues were often mentioned at Hope Baptist and New Life while I was observing these congregations, even in Sunday worship. Pastor Johnson criticized the Christian Right during one Vineyard service for its narrow focus on traditional family values. He said that "some well-meaning people are idolizing the family" and suggested that attention to "family values" was a misguided effort to "insulate their children from the world" (field notes, March 20, 1994). The comment was subtle but clearly critical of the conservative wing of evangelical Protestantism.

Kennedy reports that only 1 in 6 Anaheim members insists on traditional gender roles ("a women's place is in the home"), but he finds that 98 percent believe that homosexual relations are morally wrong and that only 4 percent agree that abortion should be legal regardless of the reason. By these measures, the Vineyard is fairly liberal on gender role preferences but conservative on sexuality.

Midwest Vineyard has what it calls a Living Waters Ministry, described as "a ministry of God's healing power to homosexual strugglers." "We don't claim to have any quick fix remedies for the homosexual struggler," ministers say, "but by embracing the process of change, Scripture promises greater sexual wholeness." The goal is to replace a "sexually confused identity with a Christian one," but the Vineyard approach is more compassionate than condemning. It seeks to persuade others by example rather than labeling and persecuting deviants. There were no warnings during Sunday worship about the evils of homosexuality, and there was only one brochure on abortion on a vast literature table outside the auditorium. It was a well designed brochure for Northside Crisis Pregnancy Center, a "prolife" Christian organization, but its approach was soft-sell. There were no prolife newsletters at Vineyard services and no fliers advertising protest actions at local abortion clinics.

Vineyard members may uniformly oppose abortion and disapprove of homosexual relations, but that is not why they attend this church. These are tangential issues in the lives of most congregants. Midwest Vineyard has not married a homosexual couple, nor does the church purge homosexuals from its membership, though it clearly takes the position that homosexuality is wrong because it violates scripture. However, on other issues the Vineyard is quite liberal, falling somewhere between the Southern Baptist and Calvary Chapel congregations previously discussed. The most significant thing about the morality of Vineyard members is not their stand on any particular issue but their outlook on moral questions generally. Their Sunday morning message is consistently one of tolerance toward others rather than judgment. Two teachings exemplify this position.

On March 20, Pastor Johnson gave a teaching on judgment from the Gospel according to Luke:

> Do not judge, and you will not be judged. Do not condemn, and you will not be condemned. Forgive, and you will be forgiven. (6:37–39)

And the accompanying parable:

> Why do you look at the speck of sawdust in your brother's eye, and pay
> no attention to the plank in your own eye. How can you say to your
> brother, "Brother, let me take the speck out of your eye," when you your-
> self fail to see the plank in your own eye. You hypocrite. First, take the
> plank out of your own eye and then you will see clearly to remove the
> speck from your brother's eye. (6:40–42)

The entire forty-five-minute teaching was devoted to an explication of these
passages. Johnson told the congregation that it is essential for Jesus' disciples to
avoid judgment because the consequences of it are serious. To begin with, people
don't have the authority to condemn, he said; only God does. Furthermore, if
we do judge others, we will be judged by them. But most important, he said, if
we are busy counting the sins of others who do not meet our exacting expectations, then we cannot see the work of God around us because our hearts are
clogged up with an attitude of judgment, like the hearts of the Pharisees who
could not see the miracle of Lazarus because they were preoccupied with viola-
tions of the law (field notes, March 20, 1994). This criticism of judgment is
striking, together with the absence of any reference to "family values" during
worship.

   Paul Lucas, the executive pastor, preached a similar message on judgment
a month later. His teaching drew on John 8:1–11 and was explicitly about
sexual immorality, but the message was about forgiveness, not condemnation.
The Gospel passage reads as follows:

> Then everyone went home, but Jesus went to the Mount of Olives. Early
> the next morning he went back to the Temple. All the people gathered
> around him, and he sat down and began to teach them. The teachers of
> the Law and the Pharisees brought in a women who had been caught
> committing adultery, and they made her stand before them all. "Teacher,"
> they said to Jesus, "this woman was caught in the very act of committing
> adultery. In our Law Moses commanded that such a woman must be stoned
> to death. Now, what do you say?" They said this to trap Jesus, so that they
> could accuse him. But he bent over and wrote on the ground with his
> finger. As they stood there asking him questions, he straightened up and
> said to them, "Whichever one of you has committed no sin may throw
> the first stone at her." Then he bent over again and wrote on the ground.
> When they heard this, they all left, one by one, the older ones first. Jesus

was left alone, with the woman still standing there. He straightened up and said to her, " Where are they? Is there no one left to condemn you?"

Lucas's interpretation of this lesson is striking. He told the congregation that in twenty-two years he had never preached on this passage from the Bible, and moreover, many churches, including the fundamentalist church he was raised in, avoid this scripture lesson because they do not want parishioners to think that grace is cheap. The Pharisees are not really concerned about sexual immorality, Lucas said; they are trying to trick Jesus into publicly violating the law so as to justify their persecution of him. Pastor Lucas said that Jesus did not violate the old law—adultery is wrong—by disagreeing with the Pharisees. Rather He introduced a new law—all sins are forgiven; grace is extended to everyone. Lucas then told a story about a woman who had an abortion and later regretted the decision. He said, in effect, that we all make mistakes, and we are all forgiven. There is right and wrong conduct in the eyes of God, but the highest Christian duty is to love others, not to judge them. No doubt this is a comfortable message for people whose experience, by virtue of their generational membership, has led them across the boundaries of right Christian conduct as defined by an earlier generation of evangelical Protestants.

Kennedy's work included a nationwide survey of Vineyard pastors. More than half are between the ages of thirty-five and forty-five, and half were reared in evangelical churches. He found that, prior to becoming Christians, 39 percent had abused alcohol often, and another third had done so occasionally. One-forth had used marijuana or other illegal drugs often; another quarter had done so occasionally. And almost two-thirds had engaged in premarital sex, 26 percent saying they had often done so (1992, 11–14). Vineyard members are not moral relativists, but they are tolerant of individual differences, for obvious reasons.

Two other factors further signify this extraordinary cultural openness. The first is a new version of ecumenism, and the second is what Vineyard calls "cultural currency." Midwest Vineyard is not part of the old ecumenical movement, but it embodies some of that spirit in new form. Among the things Vineyard values, according to its statement of faith, is "unity." "We are convinced," Vineyard members say, "that all who belong to Christ are one in his Body, the Church. We aim to maintain unity by honoring all who call on Jesus' name and by reconciliation with all parts of the Church." This is not an interfaith movement, and while its adherents share certain demographic and cultural characteristics with New Age groups, it is not a universalistic faith; Vineyard congregants remain evangelical Christians, but they cooperate with other churches in the community.

On Good Friday, for example, Vineyard held an evening service at the First Baptist Church and used the opportunity to baptize several new members. The church sponsors an occasional weekend coffee house at the Congregational church, hosts college volleyball picnics with the Presbyterians; and often holds Sunday evening meetings at the United Methodist Church. As indicated earlier in this account, Vineyard draws on a variety of resources for doctrinal literature, which tends to come from evangelical quarters (for example, the Presbyterian publishing house for money matters, International Church of the Foursquare Gospel for instruction on the gifts of the Spirit, and Inter-varsity Christian Fellowship on Christology). Kennedy found that nearly three-fourths of the Anaheim Vineyard members say that someone who is against all churches and religion should nevertheless be allowed to make a speech in their city (1992, 7).

Vineyard states boldly that it values being culturally current. It reflects this through using worship music that is of a popular style. "We aim," a brochure says, "to develop an atmosphere of ease to speak, act, and dress in ways in which this present generation can readily respond positively."

In short, Vineyard is liberal on some social issues and conservative on others, but its disposition toward alternative moralities is consistently marked by tolerance. Because Midwest Vineyard's beliefs and practices are so contemporary, it deviates from those of most conservative Protestant congregations. New-style evangelicalism embraces many elements of secular culture that were offensive to an earlier generation of evangelicals. Yet its churches remain doctrinally conservative and thus represent an innovative form of born-again Christianity that weds traditional theology and contemporary culture: members celebrate a personal relationship with Jesus Christ and talk on cellular phones; they believe in miracles and value modern science; they interpret scripture literally and shop at The Gap; they are committed to evangelizing the world yet show a remarkable tolerance for cultural diversity. Moreover, because this unexpected combination of theological conservatism and social liberalism is resulting in rapid membership growth nationwide, these findings have important implications for the debate about *which* churches are growing and *why*.

Resurgent Evangelicalism and the Vineyard Movement in Context

The basic pattern of religious change in the United States is clear. For three decades, liberal Protestantism has been in decline while conservative Protestants—evangelicals—have increased in number. Moreover, conventional wisdom says that conservative churches grow because they are conservative ("strict"), and liberal churches are declining because they are liberal ("lenient") (see Kelley 1972, Finke and Stark 1992, and Iannaccone 1994). This explanation of church growth is consistent with Kai Erikson's (1966) insight on the community-enhancing function of deviance. Conservative Protestantism makes strong behavioral demands on members, requiring them to give up alternative forms of gratification for a "Christian life." Those who fail to make sacrifices and live up to the group's high standards are ostracized. Because the cost of affiliation is high, membership is more valuable to individuals, the argument goes, making conservative churches stronger institutions. One would predict, then, that groups with clear moral boundaries would fare better in the religious marketplace because they demand more from individual members: that is, conservative (or strict) churches grow.

While these generalizations are more or less accurate *descriptions* of aggregate church membership trends—Baptists have outgrown Presbyterians and Congregationalists in recent decades, for example—the emergence of new evangelical organizations like the Vineyard, religious groups that are not clearly liberal or conservative, calls for a reevaluation of received wisdom on which churches grow and why, for two specific reasons.

First, church membership data—supplied to researchers by denominational offices (see Bradley et al. 1992)—will not include information on new, independent, and innovative religions, and because nondenominational churches may be the fastest-growing segment of American religion, this poses a serious problem. Thus Vineyard and similar religious organizations are excluded from my analysis of aggregate church membership trends. Together, groups like Vineyard and Calvary Chapel constitute a fellowship of several hundred thousand members nationwide. And while it is true that most nondenominational churches are evangelical, they are not necessarily conservative.

This, then, is the second problem with conventional wisdom on church growth and decline. Not all evangelical churches are alike in efforts to keep tradition and relate to the wider culture. Some are more resistant to social change than others and hence more strict in their enforcement of their moral standards. Maintaining boundaries between themselves and the wider culture by enforcing strict codes for moral behavior is not always the chief concern in evangelical communities. In fact, it may be less relevant for understanding evangelical growth today, more than twenty years after the "strict churches grow" thesis was first advanced, despite recent overtures by the Christian Right.

In the 1960s and '70s, as Kelley observed, the Southern Baptist Convention was healthy and growing compared to the Presbyterians or the United Church of Christ, for example. There is, however, growing evidence that oldline evangelicals, like Southern Baptists, while still outperforming liberal Protestants in aggregate membership terms, are no longer the driving force behind the resurgence of born-again Christianity. New-style evangelicalism can claim the fastest-growing churches today, and the most distinctive thing about the new evangelicals is not their strictness with regard to contemporary culture but rather their increasing tolerance of it. Indeed, Vineyard may be growing precisely because it is culturally current, compared to evangelical alternatives that continue to resist the liberal drift of modern American society.

The Californication of Conservative Protestantism

This metaphor—the Californication of conservative Protestantism—has two meanings, one demographic and the other cultural. The Vineyard Christian Fellowship, and groups like the Vineyard, started in Southern California and are growing throughout the United States by sending out missionaries to plant churches and by taking independent congregations of like mind under their associational wing. California is an important site for the revitalization of evangelical Protestantism in recent decades, and as the Vineyard case illustrates, resurgent evangelicalism is driven in part by the eastward spread of born-again Christian organizations based in the West. But California is also a place where evangelicalism is being transformed. The social and cultural liberalism of the new evangelicals is, from the perspective of conservative Christians, a perversion of tradition—a Californication of evangelical Protestantism.

The cultural changes under way in churches like Midwest Vineyard are quite radical. Vineyard's accommodation to the wider culture is more than just a change in the dress code. Its born-again Christians are embracing many of the worldly mores their evangelical forebears strenuously resisted, such as drinking, dancing, and divorce. These new evangelical communities, of course, still have moral boundaries, but they are much more permeable, and they respectfully acknowledge the diversity of cultures in contemporary life to a far greater degree than do old-line evangelical churches.

If Miller and Kennedy (1991) are right that the continued vitality of a religious institution is contingent on its achieving a "cultural fit" between its constituents and the beliefs and practices it promulgates, then fundamental changes in evangelical culture should not be surprising. Nor should the fact that evangelicalism is being transformed on the sunny shores of Southern California, which has a long history of playing a lead role in cultural innovation. However, if the movement is significant in broad cultural terms, then it will need to show appeal and staying power outside the West, and Midwest Vineyard is a striking example of the transformation of evangelicalism in the heartland.

Of course, some southern churches are still growing, even outside the South, and churches like Vineyard and Calvary Chapel are relatively small movements compared to the Southern Baptist Convention. Thus generalizations about contemporary evangelicalism based on these new churches are dangerous. Data from the General Social Survey—a more representative sample of the U.S. population as a whole—can be used to identify the social correlates of evangelical preference. Unfortunately, because Vineyard and Calvary are new and relatively small, they are not well represented in national survey data, but it is possible to compare religious change both in and outside the South, which is yet another way to explore the causes and consequences of resurgent evangelicalism.

Part IV

Why Some Evangelical Churches
Are Growing

CHAPTER SEVEN

Regional Variation in the Social Sources of Contemporary Evangelicalism

The study which we are undertaking [in *Elementary Forms*] is . . . a way of taking up again, but under new conditions, the old question of the origin of religion. . . . What we want to do is to find a means of discerning the ever-present causes upon which the most essential forms of religious thought and practice depend.

Emile Durkheim

Evangelicalism's continued vitality in the waning years of the twentieth century seems to be related to its ability to accommodate popular culture, to transform old-time religion. A new style of evangelical Protestantism is emerging across the United States, a trend not captured in aggregate church membership data because it is so recent and the churches involved are nondenominational.

We have seen how evangelicalism has become available to a national population, considered the challenge southern religion faces outside the South, and determined that cultural currency—the fit between religious tradition and the social surround—is critical to evangelicalism's continued growth, but we still have not shown *why* people not reared in a conservative Protestant tradition choose to join an evangelical church. How are evangelicals different from other Protestants, and what do successful new congregations offer parishioners that is absent in established churches?

My field work suggests that, beyond ascriptive ties, people affiliate with evangelical congregations because those religious institutions meet certain of their social and psychological needs more readily than other Protestant churches do. They provide community and "plausibility structures," to borrow a term from Peter L. Berger (1967). But while evangelical churches tend toward a theologically conservative worldview, that outlook is not necessarily what motivates people to join. In fact, the most vital evangelical churches today are surprisingly open to diverse lifestyle choices, thus distinguishing themselves from an old-time religion not theologically but culturally. The new evangelicals strive to meet the needs of modern individuals rather than condemning secular culture. In other words, they are essentially service oriented, social and spiritual filling stations. The new evangelicals do not condemn secular culture; they are not a coherent, reactionary social movement. They resemble early-twentieth-century fundamentalism less than they resemble culture-affirming organizations.

H. Richard Niebuhr has made the observation that affiliation with a Protestant denomination is not just a matter of individual choice; it has roots in the structure of society. In particular, he observed that social-class standing is causally related to the sect–church distinction in Protestantism. Sectarian movements in nineteenth-century America (Baptists, Methodists, Disciples, and the Holiness and Pentecostal movements), he argued, drew their strength from disenfranchised and culturally marginal subpopulations—frontier folk, immigrants, the urban poor, black slaves, and the like. The pews of "establishment" churches (Episcopalians, Presbyterians, Congregationalists), on the other hand, were filled with middle- and upper-middle class white people who were part of the dominant culture. Niebuhr wrote that "the divisions of the church have been occasioned more frequently by the direct and indirect operation of economic factors than by the influence of any other major interest of man. . . . [And that] economic stratification is often responsible for maintaining divisions which were originally due to differences of another sort" (1965, 26).

Yet recent research shows that while social-class differences persist, evangelical Protestantism has earned new middle-class respectability throughout the country (see Hunter 1983, especially chapters 4 and 6; and Roof and McKinney 1987, chapter 4). Moreover, with the erosion of ascriptive social ties and the blurring of class differences in the twentieth century, Americans' religious preference has become more a matter of individual choice than an expression of belonging to social groups. Roof and McKinney (1987, chapter 2) describe this as the "new voluntarism"; Hammond (1992) calls it greater "personal autonomy." Whatever it is called, this ethic is in fact what governs participation in the new evangelical churches, a point I will return to in the concluding chapter. Nonetheless, following Niebuhr's analytic strategy, it is possible to identify a constellation of social factors that, along with social status, shape individual preference for evangelical Protestantism. Religion remains, after all, a social phenomenon, and thus differences in religious belief and style of worship are explicable in sociological terms.

Indeed, the causal direction of Niebuhr's thesis—echoing classic European social theory—is that social-class background shapes the form and content of an individual's religious life: economically impoverished people are more likely than others to engage in emotional, fundamentalistic, and otherworldly styles of religious behavior because their rewards in this life are few. Yet over the past several decades evangelicalism has attained middle-class standing. (It is common in places like Orange County, California, to spot a late-model Cadillac sporting a bumper sticker that reads, "In Case of Rapture, This Car Will Be Driverless.") How much has postwar affluence diminished the relationship between social class and denomination? Is class standing still a "source" of church affiliation in the United States, or is resurgent evangelicalism anchored elsewhere in the social structure?

Perhaps other factors rooted in the modern experience—absence of community involvement and moral relativism, to name two (see Berger 1973 and Bellah et al. 1985)—are major sources of evangelical preference and thus a way to understand its current resurgence.

For this chapter I used pooled survey data from the National Opinion Research Center (NORC). Because several items relevant to the analysis (for example, refined denominational codes and certain morality items) were not included in NORC's General Social Survey prior to 1983, only the years 1983–90 were used. Specific denominational preferences have been recoded by NORC into fundamentalist, moderate, and liberal categories (Smith 1990). This classification corresponds closely to the one used in chapter 2, "fundamentalist" being roughly equivalent to our "evangelical" category.

Since African Americans have a radically different social, political, and cultural history from white Americans, the former group has been omitted from the following analysis. Though this results in a loss of information, combining blacks and whites in the population pool would confound efforts to identify the social sources of resurgent evangelicalism if that is defined as southern-style religion as exemplified by Jerry Falwell's Liberty Baptist Church in the 1970s and early 1980s and the new-style evangelicalism exemplified by Chuck Smith's Calvary Chapel or Bill Hybel's Willow Creek Community Church in the late 1980s and early 1990s. While there are some blacks and other non-white members in these congregations, they are predominately "white" churches, and the Christian Right—the political dimension of the southernization of American religion—is largely a white phenomenon.

Since we want to understand why people prefer evangelical to nonevangelical churches, the studied population is composed entirely of white individuals identifying themselves as Protestant, and the dependent variable is denominational preference—evangelical vs. "mainline." The following table presents a breakdown of Protestant preference for the country as a whole and by region.

116   Resurgent Evangelicalism in the United States

TABLE 7.1

Frequency Distribution of White Protestants in the General Social Survey, by Protestant Type (Pooled Data, 1983–1990)

Protestant Type*	Freq.	%	By Region South Freq.	%	Nonsouth Freq.	%
Evangelical	3,299	54%	1,582	66%	1,717	46%
Moderate	1,080	18%	238	10%	842	23%
Liberal	1,707	28%	572	24%	1,135	31%
	6,086	100%	2,392	100%	3,694	100%

*(non-Protestants $n=4,093$)

Slightly more than half of all white Protestants (54 percent) identify with evangelical churches. That figure is 66 percent in the South and 46 percent outside the South. Our concern here is the origin—in Durkheim's sense, the "ever-present causes"—of contemporary evangelicalism, particularly outside the South, where that tradition has not heretofore been dominant.

Social Class and Contemporary Evangelicalism

What is known about the social-class character of contemporary American evangelicalism? Using survey data from 1979, Hunter finds some class differences between the two Protestant camps he identifies as evangelical and liberal, which correspond roughly to Niebuhr's sect–church dichotomy and to the evangelical–mainline distinction employed here. He observed, for example, that 16 percent of all liberal Protestants had household incomes of $25,000 or more, compared to only 7 percent of the evangelicals. Similarly, 17 percent of the liberals were employed in "professional" occupations, compared to 8 percent of the evangelicals, and the percent having at least some college education was one-third compared to one-quarter for the two Protestant groups respectively (1983, 54). Roof and McKinney found similar class differences in their comparison of liberal and conservative Protestant groups (1987; see especially pages 112–13), and my research agrees. I find a 10 percentage point difference between evangelical and mainline Protestants who have household incomes greater than $40,000 (in 1986 dollars). Evangelicals are less well off. I find similar differences with education and occupation measures. But the Niebuhr thesis suggests that social class plays a *causal* role in shaping Protestant denominationalism. How, then, does socioeconomic status *affect* Protestant church preference?

The relationships among several socioeconomic indicators and evangelical church affiliation in this population of Protestants are presented in Table 7.2. I find that as income goes up, the likelihood a person will affiliate with an evangelical church systematically goes down. This pattern holds for occupational prestige (which is not reported in Table 7.2): 65 percent of all blue-collar workers (craftsmen, laborers, operators, service people) are affiliated with evangelical churches, compared to 50 percent of all white-collar workers (professionals, managers, and clerical workers). Likewise, educational attainment is inversely related to evangelicalism. Whereas three out of four people with less than an eighth-grade education prefer evangelical churches, that proportion decreases systematically as education increases. (Highly educated people, those with some postgraduate work, affiliate with evangelical churches at a rate of only 39 percent). Finally, a subjective measure of social class is also clearly inversely related to affiliation with an evangelical church. While two-thirds of all those considering themselves "lower-class" are affiliated with evangelical churches, that proportion drops as social class increases. Forty-two percent of all "upper-class" Protestants are evangelical. In short, notwithstanding evangelicals' higher social status, if we know people's class background we are

TABLE 7.2

Percent of Protestants Affiliated with Evangelical Churches Decreases as Income, Education, and Class Status Increase

Income in Thousands						
$0–10	$10–20	$20–30	$30–40	$40–50	$50–60	$60+
65%	57%	56%	56%	53%	46%	43%
(606)	(735)	(650)	(535)	(304)	(218)	(353)

Years in School					
0–7	8–11	12	13–15	16	17+
74%	65%	56%	52%	38%	39%
(255)	(953)	(2,127)	(1,240)	(667)	(477)

	Class Status		
Lower	Working	Middle	Upper
66%	63%	47%	42%
(232)	(2,476)	(2,763)	(179)

still better able to anticipate whether they are likely to belong to an evangelical or a mainline Protestant church. Even so, this information is not particularly helpful for understanding why evangelicalism is *growing* in popularity, only for showing that the historic relationship between social class and Protestant preference, while perhaps diminishing, has not disappeared. If the explanatory power of social class is diminishing, then we must look elsewhere to understand evangelicalism's resurgence.

Church of the Disinherited

Perhaps we can salvage Niebuhr's basic insight and increase our understanding of resurgent evangelicalism if the concept of disenfranchisement—central to the Niebuhr thesis—is expanded to include social and cultural as well as economic factors.[1] After all, evangelicalism in the 1980s, as it gained middle-class currency, was less inclined to preach against material gain than it was to condemn the erosion of norms governing sexuality, which it traced to the breakdown of the traditional family unit and the disappearance of a Christian ethic in the culture at large. The primary agenda of Pat Robertson's Christian Coalition, for instance (like that of Jerry Falwell's Moral Majority during the 1980s), is to stop abortion and pornography, define homosexuality as abnormal behavior, fight evolutionary theory in the public school curriculum, and preserve traditional gender roles in the family. These modern-day fundamentalists have become vocal and increasingly political because they feel threatened by the absence of traditional Christian morality in the cultural fabric of the United States. The preservation of "family values" is thus treated, de facto, as the "cause" of evangelical renewal by those in American society perplexed by the apparent revitalization of old-time religion. That is, because evangelicals have been increasingly visible in American civic life as defenders of traditional Christian values, their growth is thought to be the result of successfully gathering in those who sympathize with their moral agenda. This seems plausible, and certainly it is consistent with the southernization thesis—conservative Protestantism is growing outside its traditional social base. But is it true? Is rebellion against cultural change the basis for growth?

Unfortunately, cross-sectional survey data do not allow a definitive test of this hypothesis. I cannot know, for example, whether people were morally conservative and therefore became born-again Christians or whether cultural conservatism is a religious consequence or simply associated with evangelical church affiliation. The same is true for my measures of socioeconomic status, though it

---

1. In fact, Niebuhr does so by attending to region and race differences in American culture. Region is a key variable in my analysis, but I introduce it later in the chapter as a control variable rather than an explanatory variable.

is easier to imagine these factors as antecedents to, not consequences of, religious preference. I can observe empirical relationships between social class and denominational preference, but any causal direction—*how* these things are related—must be specified in theory.

Likewise, I can show that moral traditionalists disproportionately prefer evangelical churches, which is not news, but are moral issues really a *source* of evangelical growth? I think not. There is no clear evidence in my field work in either southern churches or the new evangelical churches to suggest that people join primarily for ideological reasons. True, when relocated southerners join a Baptist church outside the South, as many have, they are expressing cultural preferences—including moral preferences—but that does not explain the absolute growth of evangelicalism in recent decades (that is, the large number of newcomers to the faith). When nonsoutherners and those reared outside conservative Protestant traditions join evangelical churches, they appear to do so because those institutions attend to personal needs first and foremost, not because they offer a social reform agenda. Certainly most who join an evangelical congregation will become comfortable with church doctrine if they stay in that congregation, but, while the relationship between cultural traditionalism and preference for evangelical churches definitely indicates something of the meaning of contemporary evangelicalism, it may not be the best explanation for the renewed vitality of born-again Christianity. Moreover, the conservative revolution thesis fails to account for the relatively slow growth in southern churches compared to the rapid growth of new-style evangelicalism in Central Coast, California, and elsewhere. The following causal model (see below, "An Explanatory Model of Evangelical Church Preference") shows a more plausible explanation for the resurgence and meaning of contemporary evangelicalism in areas outside the South.

An Explanatory Model of Evangelical Church Preference

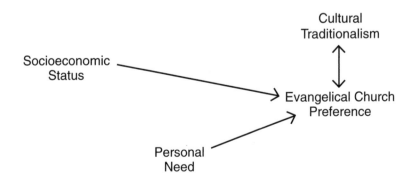

This model treats cultural traditionalism as a critical feature of contemporary evangelicalism but not the primary source of its resurgence outside the South. New members may sympathize with the cultural agenda, and they may even come to find a strict moral and theological code reassuring, but converts come into the church initially because it helps them deal with personal crises, *particularly if those individuals lack other kinds of social support.* The heavy emphasis on personal ministry in churches like Vineyard and Calvary—evident in programs that support everything in a person's life from financial concerns to drinking problems and recreational activities—is the latest manifestation of this role that evangelical churches have played exceptionally well in American history.

Of course, personal crisis is not new to modern life, but crisis in the absence of a supportive community, it might be argued, is relatively new, creating a need that evangelical churches exploit better than other Protestant groups do. Therefore, I think personal need is the critical variable to understanding resurgent evangelicalism. People in crisis who are without community, in areas where evangelical religion is not "established" and conventional, are more likely to affiliate with evangelical churches, particularly if their social background does not predispose them toward so-called mainline denominations of nonsouthern society.

An argument for this thesis begins with a consideration of the relationship between cultural traditionalism and resurgent evangelicalism. Cultural conservatives—those most uncomfortable with moral relativism—are drawn to evangelical churches because those institutions resist the liberal drift of mainstream culture; they provide a kind of moral refuge in a changing cultural environment, the argument goes. Indeed they do, and theological certainty—the belief in an ordered universe with God at the helm—is often taken as the reason people attend evangelical churches. "Because they preach the truth," one Calvary member said when asked why she attends that church and not another. Yet does it follow that moral traditionalism motivates people to join an evangelical church, perhaps even switch from a liberal one? The political wing of resurgent evangelicalism in the 1980s certainly articulated that faction's crusade in those terms, but its leaders (Falwell, Robertson, Bakker, Swaggert, and others) were evangelical by birthright—that is, they were reared as southern conservatives. Whether or not those outside the South who have become born-again Christians in recent years have done so to protest the disappearance of a familiar moral culture is a different issue.

To explore the relationship between moral issues and evangelical church preference, I constructed an index of cultural traditionalism by combining answers to five survey items on morality. The questions were designed to gauge respondents' sentiments about abortion, homosexuality, premarital sex, traditional gender roles, and the role of religion in public schools. All items were coded so that a score of 1 indicates a traditionalist perspective and a score of 0 indicates sympathy for the new morality. To generate the index, I summed up respondents' scores on all five items; thus the index ranges from 0 to 5. Item wording is as follows (traditionalist response indicated):

(1) Abortion: A pregnant woman should *not* be able to obtain a legal abortion if she became pregnant as a result of rape.

(2) Homosexuality: Sexual relations between two adults of the same sex is always or almost always wrong.

(3) Premarital Sex: If a man and woman have sex relations before marriage, it is always or almost always wrong.

(4) Woman's Place: Women should take care of running their homes and leave running the country up to men.

(5) School Prayer: Disapprove of the U.S. Supreme Court ruling that no state or local government may require the reading of the Lord's Prayer or Bible in public schools.

Table 7.3 shows that a traditional perspective on moral issues is strongly related to a preference for evangelical churches. As the index of cultural traditionalism increases, the proportion of Protestants affiliated with evangelical churches rises (from 33 to 81 percent), and the pattern holds both inside and outside the South. Even though cultural traditionalists disproportionately affiliate with evangelical churches in both regions of the country, however, I remain agnostic on the *causal* significance of moral issues as an explanation of resurgent evangelicalism, for good empirical reasons.

Moral conservatives prefer evangelical churches irrespective of region, according to Table 7.3. Yet if people are joining evangelical churches primarily to voice their disapproval of a liberal shift in American culture, then one might expect evangelicals outside the South—where the resurgence of born-again Christianity is most remarkable—to uphold a traditional morality with a diligence equal to that of their religious kin in the South. That is not the case, however. There are some remarkable differences between evangelicals in and outside the South, a variation paralleling differences I found in my field work between the old-style and new-style evangelicalism.

Is all this using the FUND variable, or is it using his dever classification?

TABLE 7.3

Percent of Protestants Affiliated with Evangelical Churches Increases as the Index of Cultural Traditionalism Increases

| | Index of Cultural Traditionalism* | | | | | |
| | Liberal | | | | | Conservative |
	0	1	2	3	4	5
	33%	40	55	64	70	81
	(121)	(297)	(404)	(334)	(207)	(63)
South	41%	47	63	74	73	87
	(34)	(97)	(159)	(147)	(109)	(39)
Nonsouth	30%	37	50	55	65	71
	(87)	(200)	(245)	(187)	(98)	(24)

*This index is powerfully related to evangelicalism, but it has the following problems. First, the items in the index were not asked of respondents in each year of the GSS between 1983 and 1990. Second, in years when an item was included in the survey, it was not asked of all respondents. Therefore, I have complete index data for only 1,363 of 6,086 Protestants in the pooled sample. The omissions resulting from missing data are random and therefore constitute no systematic bias, but the small *n* of the cultural traditionalism index is a problem for multivariate analysis.

Table 7.4 shows the proportion of all evangelicals that take conservative positions on five moral issues, by geographic region. Homosexuality is the most offensive to evangelicals in both regions (92 percent in the South disapprove, 84 percent outside the South), and the violation of traditional gender roles is the least offensive (36 percent and 24 percent oppose respectively for the two regions). Opposition to abortion is ranked second, the banning of prayer in public schools third, and the immorality of premarital sexual relations fourth. It is remarkable that regional differences are substantial, and it is remarkable that there is so much variation in the degree of opposition across moral issues defined by the Christian Right as critical to their cultural agenda.

Evangelicals outside the South are more liberal on every issue by as many as 13 percentage points. Outside the South, a clear majority of evangelicals still oppose abortion and homosexuality, but only half say premarital sex is wrong, and only a quarter say a woman's place is in the home. Along with region, generational differences are critical to evaluating the meaning of contemporary evangelicalism. What is the relationship between age and evangelical preference?

TABLE 7.4

Of All Evangelicals, Percent Who Are Conservative on Moral Issues, by Region

	Inside the South ($n=1,135$)	Outside the South ($n=1,228$)	Percentage Point Diff. Between Regions
Percent who Oppose:			
Homosexuality	92	84	− 8
Legalizing Abortion	76	71	− 5
Eliminating Prayer from Public Schools	74	61	− 13
Premarital Sex	58	49	− 9
Women Working Outside the Home	36	24	− 12

Consistent with the proposition that religious conservatism is a function of age, Hunter reports that the median age of evangelicals is higher than the median age of liberal Protestants (48 compared to 45) and members of other religious groups (1983, 50). My finding that age is *inversely* related to evangelical church affiliation was therefore unexpected. According to General Social Survey data, young people are less likely than their parents to belong to a church, but if they belong, they are more likely than their parents or grandparents to affiliate with an evangelical church. Sixty percent of people in their twenties are affiliated with an evangelical church, compared to 54 percent of those in their forties and fifties and 48 percent of those in their seventies.

Table 7.5 shows the cumulative effect of region and age on the moral perspective of contemporary evangelicals. These differences help clarify how evangelicalism changes when it leaves the South and is passed on from one generation to the next. For example, 95 percent of the evangelicals in the South who are over the age of forty consider homosexuality morally wrong, compared to 81 percent of the evangelicals outside the South who are under the age of forty. There is less difference between those two groups of evangelicals in opposing abortion (80 and 71 percent respectively), but differences increase for all other moral issues. Young evangelicals outside the South are 22 percentage points more liberal on prayer in public schools then old evangelicals in the South. They are 28 percentage points more liberal on the issue of premarital sex and 27 percentage points more liberal on the role of women in the family. In sum, the critical issues among evangelicals are homosexuality and abortion rights, but tolerance for alternative moral positions on even these issues is increasing as evangelicalism spreads and a new generation fills church pews.

TABLE 7.5

Of All Evangelicals, Percent Who Are Conservative on Moral Issues, by Region and Age

	Inside the South (n=1,135)		Outside the South (n=1,228)		Cumulative Percentage Point Difference
	Old (40 and over)	Young (under 40)	Old	Young	
Percent who Oppose:					
Homosexuality	95	89	87	81	− 14
Legalizing Abortion	80	71	70	71	− 9
Eliminating Prayer from Public Schools	79	68	64	57	− 22
Premarital Sex	71	41	55	43	− 28
Women Working Outside the Home	45	25	29	18	− 27

Since evangelicals are more liberal where they are newly prosperous— among young people outside the South—these differences in moral perspective among contemporary evangelicals must be taken seriously in evaluating the meaning of evangelicalism's current resurgence. If resurgent evangelicalism is essentially a conservative backlash to cultural change, as many argue (see, for example, Faludi 1991), then these findings make little sense, for it appears that evangelicals are fairly liberal on several moral issues, and they are most liberal where they are growing fastest. However, evangelicalism itself may be changing—becoming more tolerant of alternative lifestyles—in which case its resurgence means something altogether different and its source must be located not in ideology but elsewhere in the social structure.

It is easy either to overemphasize or underemphasize the role morality is playing in the resurgence of evangelicalism because it is difficult to measure the causal effect of cultural phenomena. Thus "family values" are a prominent feature of contemporary evangelicalism, and persons upholding them are found

[handwritten: free is not a winning argument]

disproportionately to be evangelical. But personal problems—existential crises in the absence of community—are triggering events that better explain why people not reared in a conservative Protestant tradition join an evangelical church. Of course, all church communities tend to provide some social support for their membership, but evangelical churches have historically serviced individual needs particularly well.

[handwritten: ? says who?]

A born-again experience often occurs during crisis in an individual's life; for several people I interviewed, for example, religious conversion was the turning point in a protracted struggle with drug or alcohol abuse. Coming into the church thus represented for them a new form of social support—a disciplined community and a new way of thinking about right and wrong. Might it generally be true that disaffection impels people to affiliate with a church? If so, then we might expect disaffected individuals to be disproportionately affiliated with evangelical churches. However, testing this hypothesis with cross-sectional survey data presents a problem. Because churches typically care for their membership by helping them deal with personal problems (and thus reduce those problems to the degree that the care is successful), and because church membership and personal crisis are measured simultaneously with cross-sectional data, any effect found of personal need's leading to evangelical church affiliation will be residual, thus *underestimating* its causal significance. Given this measurement obstacle, any effect I do find must therefore be potentially important. None of the specific items in the General Social Survey measures "personal need" exactly as I define it, but a combination of several items approximates the concept, thus allowing an exploration of this issue.

[handwritten: NO!]

[handwritten: ?(]

That evangelicalism draws on a population of individuals who are in some sense disaffected is supported by the finding that people who are in poor physical health and who experience significant crises in their lives are disproportionately affiliated with evangelical churches. Data in Table 7.6 show that ill health more likely characterizes people who prefer evangelical churches. People with "poor" health are 10 percentage points more likely to affiliate with evangelical churches than those who say they are in "excellent" health. Furthermore, a composite measure of personal crisis shows that the cumulative effect of divorce, unemployment, hospitalization, and the death of a close friend or relative also predisposes people to affiliate with an evangelical church.[2] There is a 10 percentage point difference between those scoring high and those scoring low on the personal crisis index.

---

2. People were assigned one point on the crisis index for each of the following four conditions: recent hospitalization, current unemployment, recent divorce, recent death of a close friend or relative. The index of personal crisis ranges from 0 to 4.

TABLE 7.6

Percent of Protestants Affiliated with Evangelical Churches Is Higher for Individuals in Crisis and Those with No Social Ties

Personal Crisis Index	Low 0	1	High* 2,3,4
	51% (1,047)	52% (1,372)	61% (862)
Health	Excellent	Good/Fair	Poor
	51% (1,217)	56% (2,343)	61% (218)
Social Ties Index	Ties		No Ties
	52% (2,591)	57% (970)	63% (248)

*The high end of the crisis index was collapsed because the number of cases is small and because it simplifies subsequent analysis.

While these relationships by themselves are not particularly strong, my hypothesis is that personal crisis, in a setting of weakened or tenuous social ties, is an important cause of evangelicalism's resurgence. The weakening of ascriptive ties is a characteristic feature of modern life, and, while most modern individuals find social ties, those who have moved away from the communities they were raised in must establish new social ties. The evangelical churches growing today are those that find creative ways of providing community to individuals cut loose from ascriptive social ties. We therefore expect to find that contemporary evangelicalism draws in people who are having difficulty coping with personal hardship and tragedy especially if they have no community to support them.

In other words, we are interested in the cumulative effect of crisis (measures of personal need) and the absence of social ties. Having already a measure of personal need, I developed a second simple index to measure respondents' social ties—the degree to which people are located in community. If individuals indicate they "never" spend a social evening with others, they score 0 on the social ties index. If they spend some time—at least once a year—socializing with someone in their own neighborhood *and* someone outside their neighborhood, they score 2 on the index. If they do one but not the other, they score

1 on the index. People without social ties are 11 percentage points more likely to prefer evangelical churches than those with social ties (see Table 7.6). Again, because people who belong to a church are presumably in community, this finding must be thought of as residual—a low estimate of the effect of social ties on evangelical church preference.

Most people score high on the social ties index and low on measures of personal crisis; that is, most people lead active and stable social lives uninterrupted by crisis, but those few who do lack social ties *and* encounter crisis turn out to be more likely to affiliate with evangelical churches. Table 7.7 shows that when social ties diminish and personal crises increase, the likelihood that a person will affiliate with an evangelical church goes from 50 to 75 percent. Similarly, when social ties diminish and physical health deteriorates, the likelihood that a person will affiliate with an evangelical church goes from 48 to

TABLE 7.7

Cumulative Effect of Personal Crisis/Health and Social Ties on Evangelical Preference

			Personal Crisis		
			Low		High
			0	1	2,3,4
	Some	2	50% (377)	50% (486)	57% (267)
Social Ties		1	49% (123)	54% (168)	60% (127)
	None	0	62% (29)	60% (48)	75% (40)

			Personal Health		
			Excellent	Good/ Fair	Poor
	Some	2	48% (373)	56% (625)	67% (42)
Social Ties		1	61% (115)	56% (231)	61% (33)
	None	0	64% (22)	60% (57)	70% (23)

70 percent. Neither variable alone—personal need (measured in two ways) or lack of social ties—is strongly related to evangelicalism. Both are significantly related in the expected direction. Taken together, however, they have a substantial impact. Vulnerable individuals disproportionately affiliate with evangelical churches.

The brilliance and novelty of Niebuhr's argument at the time he made it lay in the fact that it explained denominationalism not in terms of religious doctrine but rather as a function of the structure of social life. "For if religion supplies the energy, the goal, and the motive of sectarian movements," he wrote, "social factors no less decidedly supply the occasion, and determine the form the religious dynamic will take" (1965, 27). He was after the social sources of denominationalism, and so am I. The critical explanatory question, then, is not about theology or even moral ideology per se; rather, it is this: are the disenfranchised—measured in various social-structural ways—more likely to be affiliated with evangelical rather than mainline Protestant churches? They are, as I have shown. Social class remains a source of evangelical preference, but so does personal need—that is, individual hardship in the absence of a supportive community. Yet what is the *relative* significance of personal need compared to socioeconomic status?

Tables 7.8 and 7.9 present data on the effect of personal need on Protestant preference, controlling for several social-class- background factors. Personal need is measured in Table 7.8 by an index that combines individual health condition with the absence or presence of social ties and in Table 7.9 by an index combining the level of crisis persons experience with the extent of their friendship network: health/social ties and crisis/social ties. (These items are cross-tabulated in Table 7.7.) The first block of control figures in each table shows the effect of personal need for people with low social-class background (thus predisposing them to affiliate with evangelical churches), whether this factor is measured by low income, blue-collar occupation, or self-identification as working-class. The second block is the effect of personal need on people not predisposed by social-class factors to affiliate with evangelical churches (high income, white-collar occupations, and so on). These data show that personal need affects Protestant church preference irrespective of class standing, especially where health problems exist in those whose social-class status does not predispose them to affiliate with evangelical churches.

All of these findings support the explanatory model presented in the figure above, p. 000. Social-class factors remain relevant to understanding differential preference for Protestant churches, but, in fact, individual vulnerability—defined as personal troubles in the absence of community—appears to be another critical social factor leading to participation in evangelical churches. This is relevant to understanding evangelicalism's resurgence because people experiencing

But the DV is so loosely defined!

TABLE 7.8

Effect of Health Needs on Protestant Church Preference, Controlling for Social-Class Standing
(percent who affiliate with an evangelical church)

	Health/Social Ties					
	Low 0	1	2	3	High 4	P.P.D.*
n =	373	740	295	90	23	
	48%	57%	60%	60%	70%	
					62%	+14

	Low 0	1	2	High 3,4	
Low Social Class Status					
n =	128	361	169	81	
Low Income	52%	60%	59%	60%	+ 8
Blue-Collar Occ.	44	53	56	50	+ 6
Low Education	60	61	62	66	+ 6
Working-Class	62	66	45	66	+ 4

	Low 0	1	2	High 3,4	
High Social Class Status					
n =	231	325	100	17	
High Income	45%	53%	58%	59%	+14
White-Collar Occ.	57	64	64	71	+14
High Education	39	51	52	51	+12
Middle/Upper-Class	40	50	53	55	+15

*Percentage point difference between low and high index scores.

this combination of factors are increasingly left to their own devices to find and create supportive communities. Cultural traditionalism, on the other hand, while strongly related to evangelicalism, is less clearly a source of its contemporary resurgence. In fact, those sectors of the population in which evangelicalism is growing most—among young people and outside the South— tend to be more liberal on social issues. This phenomenon differentiates evangelicals in those sectors from their parents and from their religious coun-

TABLE 7.9

Effect of Crisis Needs on Protestant Church Preference, Controlling for Social-Class Standing (percent who affiliate with an evangelical church)

| | Crisis/Social Ties | | | | | |
	Low 0	1	2	3	High 4	P.P.D.*
n =	377	609	464	175	40	
	50%	50%	56%	60%	75%	
					63%	+13

	Low 0	1	2	High 3,4	
Low Social Class Status					
n =	130	272	235	138	
Low Income	50%	53%	62%	65%	+15
Blue-Collar Occ.	49	46	53	54	+15
Low Education	52	55	62	64	+12
Working-Class	60	61	64	71	+11

	Low 0	1	2	High 3,4	
High Social Class Status					
n =	218	288	195	45	
High Income	50%	47%	50%	56%	+ 6
White-Collar Occ.	55	55	60	70	+15
High Education	49	41	42	59	+10
Middle/Upper-Class	49	43	51	59	+10

*Percentage point difference between low and high index scores.

terparts in the South. In the future, evangelicalism may be less reactionary on social issues than is the Christian Right (a movement anchored in southern culture); in fact, as I have argued, that appears to be happening already.

As social-class differences between evangelicals and mainline Protestants diminish, and as evangelicals slowly but steadily come to embrace many elements of modern American culture, including greater tolerance for alternative lifestyles, it follows that we must look beyond ideology to explain its current popularity. I found that the ability of evangelical churches to meet the personal needs of individuals, particularly those in crisis, helps explain its renewed popularity. The evangelical churches that are growing are distinguishing themselves as service-oriented congregations.

If this thesis is correct, then the "personal need" factor will be especially pronounced outside the South and among young people—exactly those populations in which evangelicalism is growing and other social factors are disappearing as sources of religious preference. Young people outside the South are relatively free of ascriptive social ties, and that makes them more vulnerable when crisis hits their lives. Unfortunately, the data available do not allow a closer look at crises and social ties (my measures are crude), so I am unable to show what I expect is the case—that "personal need" is greater outside the South. However, there are some evangelical churches emerging outside the South that address personal need as a core feature of their program; they are emblematic of this regional difference. Saddleback Valley Community Church in California is one such congregation, as is Midwest Vineyard.

Saddleback Church, said to be one of the fastest-growing congregations in the country (with an estimated ten thousand regular attenders), is located on the eastern fringe of suburban development in Orange County. This congregation of born-again Christians is barely a decade old. Among the reasons for its success are that its leader is charismatic and its style of worship fits Southern California culture—parishioners can "come as they are," and they do—but most important, Saddleback is a program-oriented church. There are programs to meet every imaginable social need from recreational fellowship (a "bicycling ministry") to crisis counseling and support (a "Life Line" for troubled teenagers and a halfway house for battered women). The church has an elaborate twelve-step ministry—"Celebrate Recovery"—that includes at least fifteen weekly support groups centering on eating disorders, codependency, chemical addiction, sexual abuse, and other problems. There are a "recycling ministry" and a "Believer's Board Computer Ministry," among many other programs. Saddleback is a full-service religious community or, as the Sunday bulletin says, "A Life Development Church." It is affiliated with the Southern Baptist Convention and pastored by a fourth generation SBC preacher, but *there is absolutely no indication during Sunday worship—in spoken word or in print—that it is a Baptist church.* The leaders who built this church intentionally distanced the congregation from that southern evangelical cultural heritage, though they remain born-again Christians who interpret the Bible literally.

The evangelical churches that seem to be growing, like Saddleback Church, not only fit the surrounding culture but also offer programs—social services—

that meet a full range of personal needs, particularly for those in crisis or in search of community. We live, after all, in a consumer-oriented culture, and churches are becoming market-savvy institutions. With the development of more sensitive measures, national surveys will begin to show that evangelical churches are growing because they meet the social needs of individuals (many with nominal religious backgrounds). That will be the evangelical calling card of the 1990s, at least for the fastest-growing segment of conservative Protestantism. The new evangelicals tend to be moral conservatives, but that is not why people go to church. Discussions about creationism vs. evolutionary theory are available, for example, but members may choose not to take part in them; the controversy is not thrust upon them.

In short, people who are socially and culturally dislocated disproportionately affiliate with evangelical churches, regardless of socioeconomic status. Contemporary evangelicalism therefore remains a "church of the disinherited," though more in social and cultural terms than economic ones. This is especially true for young people outside the South—evangelicalism's newly prosperous social base.

CHAPTER EIGHT

The Meaning of Resurgent Evangelicalism in Late-Twentieth-Century America

[W]hat is most striking about the new religious conservatism is not its numerical growth—for evangelical and fundamentalist churches have been gaining on the liberal churches throughout this century—but rather its changing cultural ethos. At one time old-style evangelicalism was passive and withdrawn, but by the mid-1980s it had emerged as a more aggressive and culture-affirming force in the nation. Being born again became more fashionable and was on its way toward becoming a shaping influence upon contemporary American life.

Wade Clark Roof and William McKinney

Resurgent evangelicalism is affecting contemporary American life, but perhaps not in the way observers anticipated in the 1980s, when televangelism and the Christian Right dominated journalistic coverage of and scholarly research on the revitalization of born-again Christianity. During that decade, all attention was focused on the possibility that evangelicalism's new currency in the culture foreshadowed the reestablishment of a traditional Christian morality in modern American society. Christian Right leadership was staunchly conservative and very vocal on social issues, especially those related to gender, sexuality, and reproduction, thus raising concern among liberals that this reaction to the cultural revolution of the 1960s and '70s was a movement of some breadth as well as depth—that is, the number of cultural conservatives inspired by Christian faith seemed to be growing. Moreover, evangelical churches were thought to be growing *because* they were "strict" and *because* people reared outside the evangelical subculture were finding that tradition's moral and theological vision reassuring in a rapidly changing world.

The thesis that evangelicalism is growing nationwide as a result of the movement of southerners themselves and the broadened appeal of their unique

133

religious culture—the southernization of American religion—provided me an opportunity to test these commonly held assumptions about the source and meaning of resurgent evangelicalism. I found that, while conservative Protestantism has moved into the mainstream of American society, and its resurgence was related initially to the spread of southern religion, the price of success appears to be cultural—if not theological—accommodation. That is, evangelicalism may be giving up southernness in order to thrive outside the South.

The Americanization of Southern Religion

Though I have demonstrated in part 1 how evangelicalism spread throughout the country and became available to a national population, I was unable to determine with aggregate data how much the spread of southern religion per se explains evangelicalism's current growth. Nor do aggregate data allow me to assess the larger meaning of evangelical resurgence—how it affects the wider culture. An understanding about *how* it has grown could be expected to explain something important about what its growth means, thus my sojourn to observe evangelical congregations outside the South.

I found southern churches outside the South that grew initially by gathering in displaced southerners. There are still southerners in those churches, and they still attend to their historic ties with southern culture—organizationally, theologically, and morally. Yet southern churches in Central Coast, California—congregations that grew in the 1960s, 1970s, and 1980s—, are no longer growing, in part *because* they are southern. Southern evangelicals are cultural as well as religious conservatives; they resist and often condemn secular trends in the wider culture.

By contrast, there are other evangelical churches in the community that have adapted to contemporary nonsouthern culture and are thriving. These evangelical congregations are growing because they have found ways to meet the existential needs of modern individuals better than other Protestant churches, not because they are "strict"; they grow by becoming more like the culture, not less. The new evangelical congregations are program-oriented. They show greater tolerance for alternative lifestyles. And though they are theologically conservative, they make relatively few demands on their membership, reflecting the relaxed cultural preferences of the baby-boom generation.

National survey data from the 1980s show, not surprisingly, that cultural conservatives tend to affiliate with evangelical churches, but because younger evangelicals and those living outside the South—precisely the segments of the population in which evangelicalism is growing—are more liberal than evangelicals in the South, I am reluctant to think of moral traditionalism as the "source" of evangelicalism's nationwide resurgence. Southern religion as it leaves the South and is passed on from one generation to the next is becoming more liberal. This phenomenon is the Americanization of southern religion.

Why "Liberal" Evangelical Churches Are Growing

Kelley argues that "strong" churches are characterized by "social strength" (that is, membership commitment, discipline, and missionary zeal), which coincides with "traits of strictness" (absolutism in belief, conformity to the point of intolerance, and fanaticism). He further argues that a strong organization that loses its strictness will also lose its strength. Strictness, he says, tends to deteriorate into leniency, which results in social weakness (lukewarm institutional commitment, a high degree of individualism, and reserve with regard to sharing beliefs with others) in place of strength (1972, 26). In sum, successful movements must make demands. The greater the demands, the more those demands will be met by commitment.

Are traits of strictness an inevitable correlate of social strength? Conventional wisdom says that they are, but fieldwork at Midwest Vineyard fails to support that hypothesis. New evangelical churches are characterized by social strength and "traits of leniency" (relativism, diversity, dialogue). Kelley doubted that this combination was possible. Vineyard members are not moral relativists, yet they are surprisingly tolerant of cultural diversity, and they are more disposed to dialogue than monologue. Robin D. Perrin and Armand L. Mauss's (1993) work on Vineyard tests the Kelley thesis through survey data. They find that while Vineyard is clearly a strong church, it is not clearly strict. Vineyard members, Perrin and Mauss find, are highly committed and eager to share the "good news" with others, but they are unwilling to claim a monopoly on truth, and they show tolerance for individual differences. Furthermore, congregants tended to say that members of their previous church were stricter than Vineyard members on items measuring absolutism, conformity, and fanaticism.

Kelley went on to say that conservative denominations "not only give evidence that religion is not obsolete and churches not defunct but they contradict the contemporary notion of an acceptable religion. They are not 'reasonable,' they are not 'tolerant,' they are not ecumenical, they are not 'relevant.' Quite the contrary!" (1972, 25). Kelley is right about the importance of social strength—that institutions need to provide meaning and engender commitment to remain healthy, but he underestimates the need for tradition to adapt to the wider culture in order to survive in the long run. Social strength is a necessary but not sufficient condition for growth. Religions need what Vineyard calls cultural currency. In a pluralistic society, strong churches will not continue to grow if their strictness moves them too far from the cultural norms that surround their institutions. Social conservatism can be self-limiting; deviance and innovation—Christian rock music, for example—are a response to social strictness.

The Meaning of Resurgent Evangelicalism

In conclusion, my findings in this study bear on at least three important issues in the sociology of American religion:

(1) how religious change happens;

(2) the meaning of resurgent evangelicalism—whether or not the "restructuring" of American religion reflects deeper changes under way in the cultural landscape of the United States; and

(3) whether or not evangelicalism's resurgence challenges the secularization paradigm that dominates modern social theory.

Southern religion has left the South and spurred the reinvigoration of evangelicalism in recent decades. Thus the answer to the first question is that religious change is, in part, a function of demographic change. But what happens to southern churches in this cultural shuffle? Perhaps the lesson here is that they transform themselves or perish. Because culture outside the South is so different from southern culture, it is difficult to imagine how churches that champion a region-specific traditional morality could ever gain ascendancy in the larger society. The religious and cultural economy outside the South is too fundamentally pluralistic and competitive for specific denominations to monopolize the market in the near future. Those evangelical churches outside the South that are growing, such as Vineyard and Calvary Chapel, are doing do so in part because of their functional if not ideological tolerance for secular culture.

The answer to the second question, then, is that the restructuring of American culture along liberal and conservative lines is a surface tremor. The deeper, more profound change in American culture, which my findings do not challenge, is the privatization—or the "disestablishment"—of Protestantism in the United States. This is consistent with the findings of Roof and McKinney (1987) and Hammond (1992). Evangelicalism is growing, but like all religion in a modern context, it is becoming less relevant as a legitimating force in public life. In this sense, we are simultaneously experiencing religious revival and further secularization: membership is up in some Protestant churches, but religion is out as a defining feature of American civic life (see Carter 1994).

Stark and Bainbridge (1985) and Finke and Stark (1992), among others, make a convincing case that church membership trends in American history ought to be understood in cyclical rather than linear terms. Their highly praised work is a critique of the traditional secularization thesis. American society is not, they contend, becoming uniformly less religious. As certain religious institutions decline, other religious movements enter the religious marketplace and supplant them. Their model is an economic one: new religious organizations grow because they outcompete established churches for rational-acting seekers; indeed, the new evangelicals are marketing geniuses. For instance, many of the new megachurches are designed on the basis of findings from careful market research and offer their suburban constituency one-stop shopping centers: parishioners can pray and pump iron or atone and aerobicize in the same place.

Stark and Bainbridge's and Finke and Stark's descriptions of religious change are accurate enough, but they fail to recognize the secularizing consequence of the privatization of religion. The social meaning of church involvement has changed, even though church membership is on the rise. It is as if the new evangelical churches know and accept their marginality in the culture and are growing precisely because they attend primarily to the therapeutic needs of individuals and not to politics in the wider society. Evangelical Protestantism outside the South is growing today by catering to the culturally hip, and in making the tradition palatable, these new born-again congregations concede moral ground. Thus conservative Protestantism is being transformed, and the perception that resurgent evangelicalism signals a reinvigoration of traditional Christian values in American culture is simply inaccurate.

Appendix A

Excluded Denominations

Following is a list of all the denominations in the Glenmary studies for which data are available in all three years that are not included in this study. The primary reason for their exclusion is size; denominations with fewer than 150,000 members are not included in my analysis. Most of the excluded denominations are evangelical, not mainline Protestant. Furthermore, some of these denominations are less easily classified as clearly southern or nonsouthern, another good reason for omitting them from this study.

Associate Reformed Presbyterian Church (General Synod)
Brethren in Christ Church
Christ Catholic Church
Christian Union
Church of God General Conference (Abrahamic Faith), Oregon, Ill.
Cumberland Presbyterian Church
Evangelical Church of North America
Evangelical Congregational Church
Evangelical Covenant Church of America
Evangelical Mennonite Brethren Conference
Friends
Mennonite Church
Mennonite Church, The General Conference
Moravian Church in America (Unitas Fratrum), Northern Province
Moravian Church in America (Unitas Fratrum), Southern Province
North American Baptist Conference
Orthodox Presbyterian Church
Christian Brethren (formerly Plymouth Brethren)
Reformed Presbyterian Church, Evangelical Synod
Seventh Day Baptist General Conference

Appendix B

The Classification of Protestant Denominations

Following is a list, by Protestant type, of all the denominations included in this study. The goal was simply to operationalize southern-style religion as distinct from other types of Protestantism. The category "Southern Evangelical Protestant" represents southern-style religion for the analysis in part 1 of this study. There may be other fruitful ways of classifying denominations; these groupings are based on the criteria outlined in chapter 2.

Southern Evangelical Protestant

Assemblies of God
Baptist Missionary Association of America
Church of God (Cleveland, Tenn.)
Pentecostal Holiness Church
Southern Baptist Convention

Nonsouthern Evangelical Protestant

Baptist General Conference
Christian Churches and Churches of Christ
Christian and Missionary Alliance
Christian Reformed Church
Church of God (Anderson, Ind.)
Church of the Nazarene
Conservative Baptist Association of America
Free Methodist Church in North America
International Church of the Foursquare Gospel
Lutheran Church–Missouri Synod
Salvation Army
Seventh-Day Adventists
Wisconsin Evangelical Lutheran Synod

Mainline Protestant

American Baptist Church in the U.S.A.
Christian Church (Disciples of Christ)
Church of the Brethren
Episcopal Church
Evangelical Lutheran Church in America
Presbyterian Church (U.S.A.)
Reformed Church in America
Unitarian Universal Association
United Church of Christ (Congregational)
United Methodist Church

Bibliography

Albanese, Catherine L. 1988.
"Religion and the American Experience: A Century After." *Church History* 57:337–51.

Ammerman, Nancy Tatom. 1982.
"Operationalizing Evangelicalism: An Amendment." *Sociological Analysis* 43:170–71.

———. 1987.
Bible Believers: Fundamentalists in the Modern World. New Brunswick, N.J.: Rutgers University Press.

———. 1990.
Baptist Battles: Social Change and Religious Conflict in the Southern Baptist Convention. New Brunswick, N.J.: Rutgers University Press.

Bailey, Kenneth K. 1964.
Southern White Protestantism in the Twentieth Century. New York: Harper & Row.

Balmer, Randall. 1989.
Mine Eyes Have Seen the Glory: A Journey into the Evangelical Subculture in America. New York: Oxford University Press.

Bellah, Robert, et al. 1985.
Habits of the Heart. Berkeley: University of California Press.

Berger, Peter L. 1967.
The Sacred Canopy. Garden City, N.Y.: Doubleday.

———. 1973.
The Homeless Mind: Modernization and Consciousness. New York: Vintage.

Berton, Pierre. 1965.
The Comfortable Pew. Philadelphia: Lippincott.

Bloch-Hoell, Nils. 1964.
The Pentecostal Movement. New York: Humanities Press.

Boles, John B. 1985.
"Evangelical Protestantism in the Old South: From Religious Dissent to Cultural Dominance." In Charles Reagan Wilson, ed., *Religion in the South.* Jackson: Mississippi University. 13–34.

Bouma, Gary. 1979.
    "The Real Reason One Conservative Church Grew." *Review of Religious Research* 20:127–37.
Bradley, Martin B., et al. 1992.
    Churches and Church Membership in the United States, 1990. Atlanta: Glenmary Research Center.
Bruce, Steve. 1989.
    The Rise and Fall of the New Christian Right: Conservative Protestant Politics in America 1978–1988. New York: Oxford University Press.
Carter, Stephen L. 1994.
    The Culture of Disbelief: How American Law and Politics Trivialize Religious Devotion. New York: Anchor/Doubleday.
Davis, James Allan and Tom W. Smith. 1994.
    General Social Surveys, 1972-1994 [machine-readable data file]. Principal investigator, James A. Davis; director and co-principal investigator, Tom W. Smith. NORC ed. Chicago: National Opinion Research Center, producer; Storrs, Conn.: The Roper Center for Public Opinion Research, University of Connecticut, distributor. 1 data file (32,380 logical records) and 1 codebook (1073 pp).
Dawidoff, Nicholas. 1995.
    "No Sex. No Drugs. But Rock 'N' Roll (Kind of)." *The New York Times Magazine.* February 5. 40.
Dayton, Donald, and Robert Johnston. 1991.
    The Variety of American Evangelicalism. Knoxville: University of Tennessee Press.
Dorough, C. Dwight. 1974.
    The Bible Belt Mystique. Philadelphia: Westminster Press.
Durkheim, Emile. 1961.
    The Elementary Forms of Religious Life. Trans. J. W. Swain. New York: Collier.
Egerton, John. 1974.
    The Americanization of Dixie: The Southernization of America. New York: Harper & Row.
Erikson, Kai. 1966.
    Wayward Puritans: A Study in the Sociology of Deviance. New York: Wiley.
Faludi, Susan. 1991.
    Backlash: The Undeclared War Against American Women. New York: Doubleday.

Finke, Roger, and Rodney Stark. 1992.
>*The Churching of America, 1776–1990*. New Brunswick, N.J.: Rutgers University Press.

Fitzgerald, Frances. 1986.
>*Cities on a Hill: A Journey Through Contemporary American Cultures.* New York: Simon and Schuster.

Flake, Carol. 1984.
>*Redemptorama: Culture, Politics, and the New Evangelicalism.* Garden City, N.Y.: Anchor Press.

Fore, William F. 1987.
>*Television and Religion.* Minneapolis: Augsburg.

Frankiel, Sandra Sizer. 1988.
>*California's Spiritual Frontiers: Religious Alternatives in Anglo-Protestantism, 1850–1910.* Berkeley: University of California Press.

Frankl, Razelle. 1987.
>*Televangelism: The Marketing of Popular Religion.* Carbondale: Southern Illinois University Press.

Furniss, Normon. 1954.
>*The Fundamentalist Controversy, 1918–1931.* New Haven: Yale University Press.

Gallup, George. 1981.
>"Religion in America." *Gallup Report* 184.

Gastil, Raymond D. 1975.
>*Cultural Regions of the United States.* Seattle: University of Washington Press.

Hadaway, C. Kirk, Penny Long Marler, and Mark Chaves. 1993.
>"What the Polls Don't Show: A Closer Look at U.S. Church Attendance." *American Sociological Review* 58: 741-52.

Hadden, Jeffrey K., and Anson Shupe. 1988.
>*Televangelism: Power and Politics on God's Frontier.* New York: Henry Holt.
———. 1989.
>*Secularization and Fundamentalism Reconsidered: Religion and the Political Order.* New York: Paragon.

Hadden, Jeffrey K., and Charles Swann. 1981.
>*Prime Time Preachers: The Rising Power of Televangelism.* Reading, Mass.: Addison-Wesley.

Hammond, Phillip E. 1983.
>"Another Great Awakening?" In R. Liebman and R. Wuthnow, eds., *The New Christian Right.* New York: Aldine. 208–28.

————, ed. 1985.
   The Sacred in a Secular Age. Berkeley: University of California
   Press.
————. 1988.
   "Religion and the Persistence of Identity." *Journal for the Scientific Study
   of Religion* 27:1–11.
————. 1992.
   Religion and Personal Autonomy: The Third Disestablishment in America.
   Columbia: University of South Carolina Press.
Harrell, David Edwin Jr. 1981.
   Varieties of Southern Evangelicalism. Macon, Ga.: Mercer University
   Press.
————. 1988.
   "The Evolution of Plain-Folk Religion in the South, 1835–1920." In
   Samuel S. Hill, ed., *Varieties of Southern Religious Experience*. Baton
   Rouge: Louisiana State University Press. 27–28.
Haslam, Gerald. 1989
   "Dust Bowl Legacy." *Los Angeles Times Magazine*. March 26, 8ff.
Hill, Samuel S. Jr. 1962.
   "The South's Culture-Protestantism." *Christian Century* 79:1094–96.
————. 1972.
   Religion in the Solid South. Nashville: Abingdon.
————. 1980.
   The South and the North in American Religion. Athens: University of
   Georgia Press.
————. ed. 1983.
   Religion in the Southern States: A Historical Study. Macon, Ga.: Mercer
   University Press.
————, ed. 1988.
   Varieties of Southern Religious Experience. Baton Rouge: Louisiana State
   University Press.
Hoge, Dean R., and David A. Roozen, eds. 1979.
   Understanding Church Growth and Decline: 1950–1978. New York: Pil-
   grim Press.
Hollenweger, W. J. 1972.
   The Pentecostals. Minneapolis: Augsberg.
Hoover, Stewart M. 1988.
   Mass Media Religion: The Social Sources of the Electronic Church.
   Newbury Park: Sage.

Hunter, James Davison. 1982.
"Operationalizing Evangelicalism: A Review, Critique and Proposal."
Sociological Analysis 42:363–72.

———. 1983.
American Evangelicalism: Conservative Religion and the Quandary of Modernity. New Brunswick, N.J.: Rutgers University Press.

———. 1985.
"Conservative Protestantism." In Phillip E. Hammond, ed., *The Sacred in the Secular Age.* Berkeley: University of California Press.

———. 1987.
Evangelicalism: The Coming Generation. Chicago: University of Chicago Press.

———. 1991.
Culture Wars: The Struggle to Define America. New York: Basic Books.

Iannaccone, Laurence R. 1994.
"Why Strict Churches Are Strong." *American Journal of Sociology* 99:1180–1211.

Johnson, G. Benton. 1991.
"From Old to New Agendas: Presbyterians and Social Issues in the Twentieth Century." In M. J. Coalter, J. M. Mulder, and L. B. Weeks, eds., *Confessional Mosaic.* Louisville, Ky.: Westminster/John Knox Press. 208–35.

Johnson, Douglas, Paul Picard, and Bernard Quinn. 1974.
Churches and Church Membership in the United States, 1971. Washington, D.C.: Glenmary Research Center.

Kelley, Dean M. 1972.
Why Conservative Churches Are Growing. New York: Harper & Row.

Kennedy, Paul. 1992.
"The Vineyard Christian Fellowship: Demographic Characteristics of Pastors and People." Paper presented at the annual meeting of the Society for the Scientific Study of Religion, Washington, D.C.

Liebman, Robert C., and Robert Wuthnow, eds. 1983. *The New Christian Right.* New York: Aldine.

Looney, Floyd. 1954.
History of California Southern Baptists. Fresno, Calif.: Southern Baptist General Convention of California.

Loveland, Anne C. 1980.
Southern Evangelicals and the Social Order, 1800–1860. Baton Rouge: Louisiana State University Press.

Marsden, George M. 1980.
    Fundamentalism and American Culture: The Shaping of Twentieth Century Evangelicalism, 1870–1925. New York: Oxford University Press.
———. 1987.
    Reforming Fundamentalism: Fuller Seminary and the New Evangelicalism. Grand Rapids, Mich.: Eerdmans.
Marty, Martin E. 1981.
    "The Revival of Evangelicalism and Southern Religion." In David Edwin Harrell Jr., ed., *Varieties of Southern Evangelicalism*. Macon, Ga.: Mercer University Press.
Mathews, Donald G. 1977.
    Religion in the Old South. Chicago: University of Chicago Press.
McLoughlin, William G., ed. 1968.
    The American Evangelicals, 1800–1900. New York: Harper & Row.
———. 1978.
    Revivals, Awakenings, and Reform. Chicago: University of Chicago Press.
Michaelsen, Robert S., and Wade Clark Roof. 1986.
    Liberal Protestantism: Realities and Possibilities. New York: Pilgrim Press.
Miller, Donald P. 1992.
    "Hope Chapel: Revisioning the Foursquare Gospel." Paper presented at the annual meeting of the Society for the Scientific Study of Religion, Washington, D.C.
Miller, Donald P., and Paul Kennedy. 1991.
    "The Vineyard Christian Fellowship: A Case Study of a Rapidly Growing Non-Mainline Church." Paper presented at the annual meeting of the Society for the Scientific Study of Religion, Pittsburgh, Pa.
Naipaul, V. S. 1989.
    A Turn in the South. New York: Vintage International.
New York Times. 1980a.
    "Ultraconservative Evangelicals a Surging New Force in Politics." Aug. 17, 52:4.
———. 1980b.
    "Christian New Right's Rush to Power." Aug. 18, 2, 7:1.
———. 1980c.
    "Evangelicals Turn to Politics." Aug. 19, 4, 17:1.
Newman, William M., and Peter L. Halvorson. 1982.
    "Updating an Archive: `Churches and Church Membership in the United States,' 1952–1980." *Review of Religious Research* 24:54–59.

Newman, William M., Peter L. Halverson, and Jennifer Brown. 1977.
"Problems and Potential Uses of the 1952 and 1971 National Counsel of Churches' Church Membership in the United States Studies." *Review of Religious Research* 18:167–73.

Niebuhr, H. Richard. 1965.
The Social Sources of Denominationalism. New York: Meridian.

Perrin, Robin D., and Armand L. Mauss. 1991.
"Saints and Seekers: Sources of Recruitment to the Vineyard Christian Fellowship." *Review of Religious Research* 33:97–112.

———. 1993.
"Strictly Speaking. . . : Kelley's Quandary and the Vineyard Christian Fellowship." *Journal for the Scientific Study of Religion* 32:125–35.

Poloma, Margaret. 1982.
The Charismatic Movement: Is There a New Pentecost? Boston: Twayne.

Pope, Liston. 1970.
Millhands and Preachers. New Haven: Yale University Press.

Presbyterian Panel. 1993.
"Executive Summary." *Presbyterian Panel*. Louisville, Ky.: Congregational Ministries Division, Presbyterian Church (USA).

Quebedeaux, Richard. 1974.
The Young Evangelicals: Revolution in Orthodoxy. New York: Harper & Row.

———. 1976.
The New Charismatics: The Origins, Development, and Significance of Neo-Pentecostalism. Garden City, N.Y.: Doubleday.

Quinn, Barnard, et al. 1982.
Churches and Church Membership in the United States, 1980. Washington, D.C.: Glenmary Research Center.

Reed, John Shelton. 1972.
The Enduring South: Subcultural Persistence in Mass Society. Lexington, Mass.: Lexington Books.

Reed, John Shelton, and Daniel Joseph Singal, eds. 1982.
Regionalism and the South: Selected Papers of Rupert Vance. Chapel Hill: University of North Carolina Press.

Robinson, W. S. 1950.
"Ecological Correlations and the Behavior of Individuals." In George Theodorson, ed., *Studies in Human Ecology*. Evanston, Ill.: Row, Peterson, Campy. 115–26.

Roof, Wade Clark. 1993.
    A Generation of Seekers: The Spiritual Journeys of the Baby Boom Generation. San Francisco: HarperCollins.
Roof, Wade Clark, and William McKinney. 1987.
    American Mainline Religion: Its Changing Shape and Future. New Brunswick, N.J.: Rutgers University Press.
Rosenberg, Ellen M. 1989.
    The Southern Baptists: A Subculture in Transition. Knoxville: University of Tennessee Press.
Shibley, Mark A. 1991.
    "The Southernization of American Religion: Testing a Hypothesis." *Sociological Analysis* 52:159–74.
———. 1992.
    "Religion in Oregon: Recent Demographic Currents in the Mainstream." *Pacific Northwest Quarterly* 83:82–85.
Shortridge, James R. 1976.
    "Patterns of Religion in the United States." *Geographic Review* 66:420–34.
———. 1977.
    "A New Regionalization of American Religion." *Journal for the Scientific Study of Religion* 16:143–53.
Smidt, Corwin E., ed. 1989.
    Contemporary Evangelical Political Involvement: An Analysis and Assessment. Lanham: University Press of America.
Smith, Tom W. 1990.
    "Classifying Protestant Denominations." *Review of Religious Research* 31:225–45.
Southern Baptist Handbook. 1992.
    Nashville, Tenn.: Sunday School Board of the Southern Baptist Convention.
Stark, Rodney, and William Sims Bainbridge. 1985.
    The Future of Religion: Secularization, Revival and Cult Formation. Berkeley: University of California Press.
Stone, Jon. 1991.
    The Boundary Dynamics of Religious Communities: The Case of American Evangelicalism, 1940–1965. Unpublished Ph.D. dissertation, University of California–Santa Barbara.
Streiker, Lowell D., and Gerald S. Strober. 1972.
    Religion and the New Majority: Billy Graham, Middle America, and the Politics of the 70s. New York: Association Press.

Stump, Roger. 1984.
   "Regional Migration and Religious Commitment in the United States."
   Journal for the Scientific Study of Religion 23:292–303.
Sweet, Leonard I., ed. 1984.
   The Evangelical Tradition in America. Macon, Ga.: Mercer University
   Press.
Tindall, George. 1976.
   The Ethnic Southerners. Baton Rouge: Louisiana State University Press.
Troeltsch, Ernst. [1911] 1976.
   The Social Teaching of the Christian Churches. Chicago: University of
   Chicago Press.
U.S. Census Data. 1986.
   "Mobility Status Between 1975 and 1980 by State of Residence in
   1980." *Geographic Mobility, States and the Nation, 1980 Census of Popu-*
   lation. Washington, D.C.: U.S. Department of Commerce, Bureau of
   the Census.
Wacker, Grant. 1984.
   "Uneasy in Zion: Evangelicals in Postmodern Society." In George
   Marsden, ed., *Evangelicalism and Modern America.* Grand Rapids, Mich.:
   Eerdmans. 25–28.
Warner, R. Stephen. 1979.
   "Theoretical Barriers to the Understanding of Evangelical Christian-
   ity." *Sociological Analysis* 40:1–9.
Wilson, Charles Reagan. 1980.
   Baptized in Blood: The Religion of the Lost Cause, 1865–1920. Athens:
   University of Georgia Press.
———. 1985.
   Religion in the South. Jackson: University Press of Mississippi.
Wimber, John. 1990.
   "Zip to 3000 in 5 Years." *Signs & Wonders Today* 13–20.
Wuthnow, Robert. 1988.
   The Restructuring of American Religion: Society and Faith Since World
   War II. Princeton, N.J.: Princeton University Press.
Zelinsky, Wilbur. 1961.
   "An Approach to the Religious Geography of the United States: Pat-
   terns of Church Membership in 1952." *Annals of the Association of*
   American Geographers 51:139–93.
———. 1973.
   The Cultural Geography of the United States. Englewood Cliffs, N.J.:
   Prentice-Hall.

Index